Adopting Alyosha

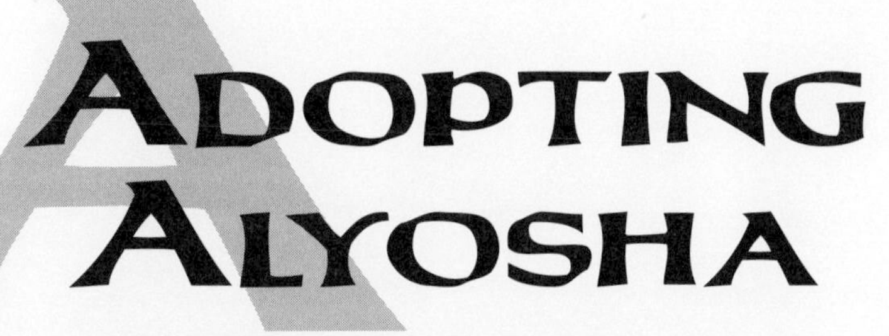

Adopting Alyosha

A Single Man Finds a Son in Russia

Robert Klose

University Press of Mississippi/Jackson

http://www.upress.state.ms.us

Many of the names in this book have been changed to protect the privacy of living individuals.

02 01 00 99 4 3 2 1

The paper in this book meets the guidelines for performance and durability of the Committee on Production Guidelines for Book Longevity of the Council on Library Resources.

Library of Congress Cataloging-in-Publication Data

Klose, Robert.
Adopting Alyosha : a single man finds a son in Russia / Robert Klose.
p. cm.
Includes bibliographical references.
ISBN 1-57806-119-9 (alk. paper)
1. Klose, Robert. 2. Intercountry adoption — United States — Case studies. 3. Intercountry adoption — Russia — Case studies. 4. Adoptive parents — United States — Biography. 5. Single fathers — United States — Biography. I. Title.
HV875.5.K59 1999
362.73'4'0973 — DC21
98-33677
CIP

British Library Cataloging-in-Publication Data available

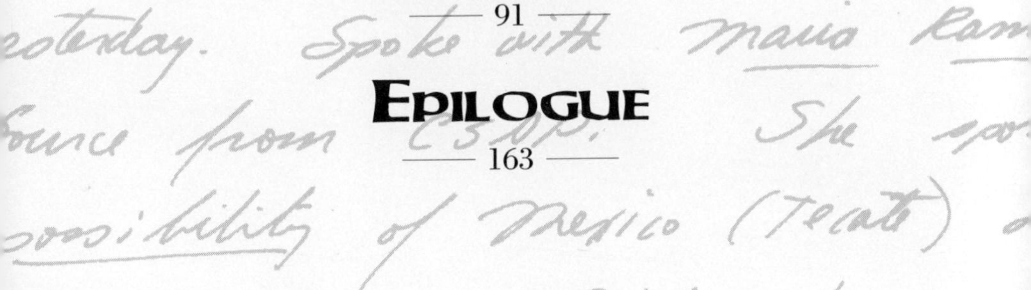

...ith all of these fellers out so...
must happen in my favor. ...
seem to be the only one dem...
this degree of optimism.

No call from Maria yet.
No call from Ray Speckt ...
Called [illegible] Unlimited in...
yesterday. Spoke with Maria Ram...
Source from CSJP. She spo...
possibility of Mexico (Tecate) ...
course, Peru. Said she would...
this week c̄ more info. ...
sudden I'm starting to se...
limited my options seem to...
single man. Peru is begin...
look like my only open door,
attractive one at that, in light...

I have never begun any important venture
for which I felt adequately prepared.

Sheldon Kopp

Adopting Alyosha

THE
WHY

I had not grown up until, at the age of thirty-nine, I adopted a child. This is not an easy statement to explain, and therefore, up to now, I have made it only to those who I felt would not ask me to.

From the time I attended the initial orientation meeting to the moment, two years later, when I was offered a little boy in Russia by an adoption agency, I kept things to myself. The false leads, the frustrations, the close calls, the agency's home visit, the interviews . . . all of these experiences belong to the subculture of adoption in the United States. I told almost no one what I was doing. I felt as if I had an alternate life, like a Mason. The only things missing were the secret handshake and the invocations.

To a greater or lesser extent, the momentous undertakings in our lives are colored and influenced by others, even if they are only onlookers. One's first car, choice of college, a decision to travel abroad, marriage—all of these things represent change; and like all change they are bound to have an effect on those family members and friends who share moments with us on our personal journeys. In a sense, I have a duty to both inform them and to allow them to participate in my plans. So why did I choose to do otherwise when it came to adoption? Why did I decide to forego as much encouragement and support as possible during a process that would be filled with a great deal of stress and frustration? (My caseworker asked me on more than one occasion, "Do you want to give up?")

I did not entirely go without. My parents and siblings knew from the start what I was up to, as did the three referents who wrote letters on my behalf. This provided both the support I needed and a degree of unsolicited advice that I could live with. But by otherwise carrying on so surreptitiously, I was operating under the conviction that adopting a child had to be all me because, for the most part, taking care of that child would be all me. In other words, I felt I had to do it alone if I was going to be able to do it alone.

I took the first solitary step on March 14, 1991, when I filled out the adoption application sent to me by my agency. I knew that, in one respect at least, I was operating from a position of strength. As a college professor, I had a decent income, a flexible schedule, and vacations in common with the grammar schools, not to mention a glorious four-month summer break during which I imagined wonderful possibilities for me and my future son. For an unmarried person, this was a powerful answer to have in my pocket when asked how I would find the time to raise a child on my own.

In fact, that question never arose. But a more fundamental one did, on the adoption agency's application: "Reason(s) for Wanting to Adopt." I was given three and a half lines in which to explain myself. This is what I wrote: "After much thought and conversations with adoptive parents, I have decided that I want to be, and am capable of being, a caring parent and role model for a child who would otherwise grow up without benefit of either."

I still think this is a good answer. (I already knew enough not to write, "Because I want to give some child a better life in America.") But I can put it much more simply now: I have long wanted to be a father and I believe I have the disposition to be a good parent.

"Disposition" is a loaded word. It contains a world of meanings: tolerance, reliability, flexibility, financial wherewithal, the ability to give and receive affection.

I have met quite a few people who desire to be parents but do not have the disposition for it. I once met a woman who told me that she wished to adopt because she wanted the pleasure of seeing a child show his gratitude for all the things she would give him.

Desire good. Disposition very bad.

So there it is. When I finally did receive my referral of a child, reactions from friends were, by and large, enthusiastic. One of the less encouraging responses was, "But you don't know what you're getting!"

This was a reference to the child's heredity.

As a biology professor, I am ever mindful of genetics, which teaches that biological children can be surprise packages as well. Mom's genes and dad's genes mingle and trade places before settling down to produce an individual with a mix of traits never before seen on the planet. Additionally, the dim echoes of deceased relatives sometimes make their way down the genetic pipeline, so that just when you thought the family had buried the memory of great-granddad Bill's terrible temper.... How is that for a surprise?

One might argue that adoptive children are *more* of a known quantity than biological children because adoptive parents get a peek at what they are being offered before giving their assent. They may even get some documentation on the child's background, which is far more informative than the foggy image of a sonogram.

I realized at the start that whether a child is biological or adopted, one does not know *all* the ingredients in the package. That is what growth is all about. A child is the slowest flower in the world, opening petal by petal, revealing the developing personality within.

I could do no more than feel forward for what could be hoped.

Accepting this as perhaps the only truth in the matter of having a child, I signed the application as an act of hope. Not the hope that my child would be brilliant or blue-eyed, agile or adept, but that he would simply be the right child for me.

The other question being begged is why a single *man* would choose to adopt. Answering "Why not?" is the easy way out, although I feel this to be an acceptable repartee. "Mother and child" is a fixed phrase. "A child without a mother" contains that plaintive note of lament aimed straight at the heart. Although the concept of what defines a family has changed in America in recent decades, our desire to constitute a family at all costs swells great within us. I was gripped by this need as well. Adoption was my opportunity to form a family of my own, and I went at it with élan. If adoption by a single man was a possibility, then I wanted to try to make it happen.

The barriers were daunting. They existed mostly in the form of adoption agencies that had little or no experience working with single men and foreign sources that simply would not accept my application. This required me to look a little harder, wait a little longer, and anguish perhaps a bit more deeply than the average prospective adoptive couple or single woman would. (Single women have a long and successful track record as adoptive parents.) I was told at the outset that the submission of an application was no guarantee of a child in the end. But hope (there it is again), if embraced long, hard, and frequently enough, gives way to conviction. Before long a vision formed in my head of what my child would look and act like, right down to his bright smile and dirty little fingernails.

Now I understand. It was not the "doing it alone" that was the mark of adulthood. It was the tentative but willful step into the unknown, the reaching out for the child who was already born and who, one day, would reveal and continue to reveal himself to me. For better *and* for worse.

As I write these words, my seven-year-old son, who is four weeks out of Russia, is leaning against my arm, yearning to peck at the keys of my computer. I am humbled by this sudden experience of having a little person at my side who wants to emulate *me,* of all people.

When I was seven, I so wanted to be a grown-up. Now that I have arrived, I can safely say that it was worth the wait.

YES
Paperwork Reduction Act
Schedule A
Part
Foreign

STATESIDE

In the Beginning

My adoption agency held information meetings "every so often," once a critical mass of interested people had accumulated. Information was not commitment. It was not even a toe in the waters of adoption. It was just a glance from afar.

My adoption agency was in Lewiston, Maine. Lewiston is one of those places on the map that one drives to but never seems to reach. The signs on the interstate always post Lewiston as being three digits away. The hundred miles might just as well have been a thousand. En route to Lewiston, my favorite FM stations decay into a harsh crackle, as if Lewiston cannot be reached even by radio wave. I had heard that adoption requires the leaping of many hurdles. Was getting to Lewiston the first of these, a test of patience and stamina?

There were moments, as I drove alone, when I could not believe I was really doing this. I mean taking the adoption bull by the horns and seeing where it would lead (or throw) me. I had even steeled myself against the eventuality that the agency would not even work with single men or that their books would be closed to new applications. If they did not want me, then that would be that, and I would be able to concentrate on my garden and catch up on my reading. But the agency had welcomed me. Making the initial phone call had been the hardest part. But once I was in my car and headed south, the idea of adoption took on a very pleasant aspect. The closer I drew to Lewiston the more anxious I was to get a look at the agency and see what they had to offer.

My anticipation grew, mile upon mile, until I repeatedly found myself traveling well above the speed limit, as if some force were occupying the passenger seat and snaking its foot over onto the accelerator. I had to make conscious efforts to ease off the gas. Lewiston will come, I kept telling myself. It must come. If I drive much longer I'll be in New Hampshire.

Then, like the Emerald City of Oz rising from the far side of an endless field of poppies, Lewiston appeared. (Please don't travel to Lewiston to verify this image.) Grateful for having at last arrived, I did not even flinch at the idea of an adoption agency operating out of a National Guard armory. It was a formidable brick building, dark and unforgiving, WWI vintage, with a steel entrance door wide enough to admit a tank.

With a thousand questions in hand, I pulled the door open and entered a long corridor: linoleum-tile floor newly buffed, dim globes for ceiling lights. My every footstep echoed. I found the office and walked in. Not a soul was there, but I was captured by a wall covered with photographs of happy families and their adoptive children who were every color of the rainbow, some visibly handicapped. My heart rose in my throat—the first time my viscera had had their say in the matter. The sound of distant voices broke my concentration.

I went back out into the corridor and followed the voices to a room holding an arc of steel folding chairs. There were six couples there, but the husbands and wives—most of them holding hands—were speaking to only one another. It was as if there were only one child in the world left to be adopted and no one wanted to lose their advantage by saying something stupid or incorrect. When I entered everyone gave me a peremptory glance. Then, in unison, they looked behind me, presumably for my spouse. My expression must have said, "There ain't no more, folks. I'm it." A moment later they turned away and resumed their quiet conversations.

I took a seat among the couples and perused my legal pad, prioritizing the questions I had brought along. I had just finished reading Lois Gilman's *Adoption Resource Book* and had dog-eared it into a Japanese fan. Although comprehensive, every page had raised as many questions as it had answered. I had dutifully jotted them down, sometimes feeling overwhelmed by the details of the adoption enterprise as well as intimidated or even frightened by some of the experiences of adoptive families.

A middle-aged woman named Janet walked in, laden with notes. As soon as she began to speak we began to scribble. She told us that the agency had been in operation for twelve years and that it had placed three hundred children, seventy percent of whom were foreign. Then she listed the steps involved in adoption:

1. **Application**
2. **Intake (interview with a caseworker)**
3. **Adoptive-parenting classes (four weeks)**
4. **Paperwork**
5. **Homestudy**
6. **Paperwork**
7. **Referral of a child**
8. **Postplacement supervision (six months to one year, depending on the age of the child)**

She added that the time frame for completion of all the paperwork was three to seven months. A child would normally be referred within a year of application.

So adoption meant a long haul. But I found comfort in this for several reasons. I would have ample time to make sure I knew what I was doing. I would be able to use the time to read, to consult with adoptive parents, and to learn as much as I could. Also, not least in importance, I would be able to save, save, save, because adoption was going to be expensive.

In fact, when Janet began to recite costs by country, I found the figures dizzying: $7500 plus travel for Honduras; $8700 plus travel for Guatemala; $10,000 plus travel for Peru; $14,000 plus travel for Chile. When she listed a mere $3000 for Thailand, my heart leaped and I circled Thailand. Before coming to the information meeting, $3000 had seemed like a lot of money. Now it was beginning to seem reasonable.

Then Janet added that Thailand was not available to singles, either male or female.

I scratched out Thailand.

Janet raised her head from her paperwork and asked if anyone was interested in Poland. "Because," she said, "if you're Catholic and of Polish ancestry you may have an advantage in adopting from that country."

"What's the cost?" I asked, being the good consumer while I made a note of the Polish option.

"We don't know yet," she said. "We've never done a Polish adoption."

Oh.

After finishing our tour of countries and listing their associated costs, Janet stated that in addition to the country fees families would be responsible for the adoption agency's fee of from $2000 to $3600, a sliding fee based on gross income.

I did some quick scribbling on my pad. More reason for hope: my teacher's income made me a solid $2000 man.

Janet opened the meeting to questions.

Silence.

There was not a single question from any of the couples. So I jumped in with alacrity.

"Do you have a payment plan?"

"Which countries are the most reliable to work with?"

"What did you mean by saying we can't choose gender?"

"What kind of support do you give us?"

"Which of the listed countries work with single men?"

"Can I have the phone numbers of some of your past clients?"

The couples were looking at me as if I had crashed their party.

Janet addressed my questions in a businesslike manner, almost like a recitation—the result, no doubt, of having been through this time and again. Mexico, she said, was considered unreliable: horror stories about couples becoming trapped down there, being bled dry, waiting for a child who might not even exist. Peru was also tricky, but doable. India was wonderful, but closed at the moment. Payment plan? Nothing sponsored by the agency, but families had been known to take out second mortgages on their homes. Single men? The agency had never "done" one, but I was welcome nevertheless.

After answering my questions, Janet went into another room to retrieve some information packets. In the silence she left in her wake, I turned to the others and asked, "Are any of you having trouble envisioning yourselves writing ten thousand dollar checks?"

No response.

Janet returned and handed out her agency's information and applications. The others seemed baffled, if not disappointed, by the whole affair. It was as if they were expecting to walk out with a child that very night. I think the talk about gender selection had been the watershed. Janet had said that families could not select the sex of their child. This immediately threw a pall over the already moribund audience. I was unaffected by this pronouncement, though. I was considering the adoption of a boy and had no illusions about a single man being given a girl. In this sense, my marital status gave me the advantage of being able to get an early start on decorating the upstairs bedroom in anticipation of a male child.

When the session was adjourned some of the couples milled about, pausing to look at albums containing photos of yet more happy, smiling adoptive children. Others approached Janet and asked questions they had been reluctant to pose in front of the others. But I felt, for the moment at least, satisfied. I was glad I had decided to come to the orientation to get my first real look at the subculture of adoption. With the information packet and application rolled up tightly in my hand, I pushed open the steel door of the armory and stepped out into the night.

I sat in my pickup under a streetlamp, while, one after the other, the couples drove away. I began to pore over the agency information and the notes I had taken. Before traveling to Lewiston I had been filled with trepidation. *Not sure. Just not sure. Have thought about it for years now, but not sure.* But as I sat in the glow of the streetlamp flipping through papers, a truth came to me. It was a good truth, something I had once read in a book. *I have never begun any important venture for which I felt adequately prepared.*

Preparedness did not mean having all the answers to all the problems that would crop up with an adoption. It meant recognizing that I had the resources within myself to respond to situations that were yet unknown and that I could not even imagine. It was all right to feel reasonably, but not fully, prepared. I was further fortified by this consideration: Why should I fail at adoption when so many have succeeded before me?

At that moment, I felt as I had while studying math in grade school. It was my hardest subject, a real conundrum for me. But the insight that came once I had solved a difficult problem gave me an unbelievable rush. It gave me the impetus to do more, to stay up a little later than I really should. I felt that way now—energetic, optimistic.

I felt as if I could drive to Lewiston and back. Five times.

Into the Woods

Intake: It sounded like something one does with a rental car, or a way to inhale an unpleasant gas.

Intake meant that I was no longer anonymous, as I had been at the information meeting, or abstract, symbolized only by my application and an attached $100 check. Now things were getting serious. I was actually being looked at as a candidate for adoptive parenthood.

It was April 1991, one month after the information session. Once again I traveled to Lewiston. Once again the road signs insisted that, despite my odometer reading, I was always a hundred-plus miles away from the city.

At the armory I met my intake worker, a pleasant, middle-aged man named Carl. (Everyone in the adoption business seems to be middle aged.) We sat opposite one another at a small, round table in a room brimming with yet more snapshots of happy adoptive families. The purpose of intake was twofold: the agency needed to find out if I knew what I was doing and if I was someone with whom they could work.

Carl was a psychologist. Little did I know that within the year he would resign from both the agency and his profession to begin a new career staging karaoke acts at local restaurants and clubs. But, for now, he was a psychologist, an amiable psychologist, not threatening in either manner or speech—no ink blots, no couch, no electrodes.

I have often thought that one would have to be an imbecile not to be able to answer a psychologist's questions correctly. I recall having taken some sort of generalized psychological exam while still in college. One of the questions was "If someone stole an item of little value to you, would it be okay to kill him?" Even if I thought that in some instances it might be okay, I would never tell that to a psychologist.

Carl's questions were cut from the same cloth, but tailored for the adoption business. I was asked, for example, if I believed in beating children to discipline them. Even if I did, the little angel on my shoulder would have whispered, "Tell him no! The answer is no, for God's sake!"

With my hands folded before me on the tabletop, I looked into Carl's eyes and told him, "I believe that if a parent needs to beat his child there is something functionally wrong with their relationship."

Carl held up his hand to slow me down. "I want to get this verbatim," he said, seeming pleased with my answer.

"What do you consider to be appropriate means of disciplining a child?" he asked as a follow-up, his pen hovering above his notepad.

The angel spoke again: "A stern look, curtailment of privileges, sending him to his room for quiet time," I enumerated, "depending on the child's sensitivity. A simple word may be enough to do the trick." Then I hastily added, "Almost anything short of a beating."

I think Carl liked me. He scribbled away with enthusiasm. I was beginning to warm to this adoption stuff.

Then Carl began to move about in his chair, appearing slightly uncomfortable for the first time. He looked at me, probing his teeth with the butt of his pen. "There's a question the director wants me to ask you."

I shrugged my shoulders and presented him with an expression of unconcern. But the little angel on my shoulder was dripping beadlets of sweat. What question, I asked myself, could be important enough to make it down the chain of command like this?

"The director wanted me to ask you why you never married."

So that was it. Gee. Carl made it sound as if I were already in a rocking chair, the subject of a retrospective on my life. "It's not as if I've shut the door to the possibility," I said, honestly.

Carl's expression continued to search.

What could I tell him? I am a very independent man who is attracted to very independent women. It is not a recipe for success. In the struggle to preserve our individual goals and habits, we eventually part to salvage a friendship, which, oddly enough, invariably persists. But did Carl need to know all this?

"I don't know," I finally offered.

Carl shrugged in a manner suggesting commiseration. Perhaps he was reflecting his own experience, saying in effect, "Women. Who knows!"

One of the last questions Carl asked me was what kind of child I was looking for. I had thought about this in the interim since submitting my application. As a speaker of Spanish who had traveled in several Spanish-speaking countries, I was endeared to those cultures and their common language. I therefore inquired about a Central or South American boy.

Age?

I had thought about this, too: four to six years old. I realized that as a single person, a baby was not really appropriate for me. Without a partner at home and with supportive family five hundred miles away in New Jersey, reality dictated that a child with some degree of self-sufficiency, that is, an older child, was best for me.

"I don't see any red flags."

That was Carl again. "Red flags" belongs to the jargon of psychologists and sociologists—warning signs. He had not detected any warning signs in my answers.

The rest of the intake interview consisted of a review of my application, questions about my family (healthy, not so wealthy, but pretty wise), and my financial resources (adequate but with little room for frivolousness). I also handed over to him proof of medical insurance, the form for which had been part of the application package.

Carl saved some of the more cogent questions for last.

What if I were to become seriously ill or die?

I had thought about this as well. My sister in New Jersey, who is married and has two young children, would care for my son in the event of my incapacitation or demise.

What did my family think of my plans?

They were supportive, very supportive. My mother was already referring to my prospective son's room as "Pablo's room."

Remember: the submission of an application is no guarantee of the referral of a child.

Carl told me he would write up the intake and hand it in for agency review. But he did not foresee any problems.

I suddenly felt that I had taken another solid step toward the child who, although he did not know it yet, was waiting for me. I felt like the sculptor who already sees the image in the block of stone: with every cleave of the chisel he comes closer to releasing it.

Still, I made overt attempts to remind myself that so much sheer bureaucracy still lay ahead. Although adoptions, by and large, come to fruition with a minimum of delay and complication and I had no reason to suspect that my situation would present me with insurmountable difficulties, the stories of scandal were rife as well. My reading about adoption was making a good consumer of me, but the anecdotes were sometimes terrifying: the couple stranded in Mexico, dependent on shady Mexican contacts who needed "just a thousand dollars more"; the couple waiting at the airport in New York for their seven-month-old Korean daughter to arrive, only to be presented with a twelve-year-old boy; the frightening isolation of going it alone in corrupt Romania. (I had read somewhere that any unscrupulous adoption facilitator, regardless of nationality, was now being referred to as a "professional Romanian.")

"No red flags," Carl repeated as he packed my case folder into his attaché. Then I handed him $500 as the first installment of the agency's fee. Writing the check had pinched a little, but handing it over was like a first seal placed on a covenant. In that act was contained, somehow, the power to make things happen in my favor.

As I drove back home that evening, I reflected that if one considered everything that could go wrong, if one read too many horror stories, if one dwelled on the potential problems without seasoning one's fears with hope, then a person would never sign on for such an undertaking. Adoption is the expectation of a reasonably happy future, with normal ups and downs. Tragedy hovers in the back of one's mind as a possibility, in the same way that people acknowledge the potential of an accident while driving. But few anticipate having one.

Intake: a pleasant gas; an opportunity for me to tell my story and have someone tell me, in turn, that I am okay.

No red flags.

What Color Is Your Harley?

I have never been much for groups. On those occasions when participation in a group has been unavoidable, I have made it clear that there are three things I will not do: state what kind of tree I would like to be, touch someone I do not know, or turn to the person next to me and tell that person that I love him.

My adoption agency required that I attend adoptive parenting classes: four hours one evening a week for four weeks. This took place two months after the submission of my initial application and one month after intake.

In Lewiston.

Carl, my caseworker, and soon to be the karaoke master of central Maine, ran the session with a helpmate, a woman named Ann.

The other prospective parents were a single woman, about forty, who had had her tubes tied when very young to prevent pregnancy from inhibiting a career that never blossomed, although a latent desire for children had. There was also a "middle-America" couple—young, bright, well-groomed: he a junior-high-school principal and she a gym instructor. Lastly there was a Harley couple. The husband, Billy, was brawny, bearded, and potbellied; had a few teeth left; and wore a T-shirt that had seen much of the world. His wife wore a frilly cotton dress and looked like the only person who could beat Billy at arm wrestling. In short, we represented prospective adoptive families from the four corners of the earth. Our portraits should have been adorning the nether regions of a medieval map.

We sat in a wide circle while Carl and Ann introduced the session. The meetings were to consist of a series of dynamics in which we were all expected to participate. There would also be a lot of direct-thought questions.

I was on edge. I was always on edge in groups. To compensate for being on edge I tended to talk a lot. And then I was on edge *because* I talked a lot, fearing I would say something that would constitute a

red flag.

But when I looked across the circle at Billy, I saw him awash in red flags, like a Soviet leader on his catafalque. So I relaxed.

The purpose of the parenting sessions was to get us to think about the most important issues pertinent to the adoption experience. There were discussions of bonding ("Do you warm to people quickly or slowly?"), disciplining children (curtailment of privileges? corporal punishment?), dealing with questions from outsiders ("What a beautiful Vietnamese baby! What language will he speak?"), and even the issue of renaming an adopted child.

The last was something I had thought about a great deal. It seemed self-evident to me that a child's name is his identity. For adopted children it may very well be the only thing that they own. Further, their name represented what most likely was their only possession from their birth country. To suddenly start calling Pablo "Harry" once he is on American soil seemed almost punitive.

For infants, of course, it is different; and some older children do ask their adoptive parents for an American name, because they want to fit in. But to foist a radical name change on an eight year old with a highly developed sense of self seems selfish, at best.

(I did get wind of one justifiable case of renaming an older child: a girl from a Middle Eastern country. Her name was originally O-Shit. It was changed to Jennifer.)

There was an interesting group dynamic that revealed how dramatically different we four adoptive parties were. It involved Carl and Ann reading a scenario involving a child's behavior and a parental response. Each of the four corners of the room represented one of the following: strongly agree, agree, disagree, or strongly disagree with the parent's reaction. Following the reading of the scenario, each adopting party was to go to the corner of the room that best represented our level of agreement with the parental action. In almost every case each migrated to a different corner, as we were consistently divergent in our opinions of what a parent should do in the situation given.

One of the scenarios was "Your two year old suddenly runs into the street. You go after him and spank him."

I went to the "strongly disagree" corner, the single woman went to "disagree," and the middle-America couple went to "agree" (although I eventually managed to lure the wife into my corner by offering a coffee mug bearing the adoption agency's logo). Billy and Candy lodged themselves solidly in the "strongly agree" corner.

Carl asked me to explain my reasoning.

"Well," I began, "you can't automatically assume that a spanking is the answer for every child. Why would that be the response of first resort? Depending on the child's level of sensitivity, a stern verbal correction might make an unforgettable impression, obviating the need for a spanking."

Billy and Candy gaped at me as if I had mistaken their bike for a Kawasaki.

Carl turned to the two of them. "What do you think, Billy?" he asked.

Billy swiped the air with his hand. "Give'm a whack on the ass. He won't run in the street again."

Silence.

At that moment I saw Billy in a different light. I think my response had been honest, but guardedly so. Higher education had taught me to wrap my reasoning in a labyrinth of prose that would discourage all but the most persistent souls from understanding me. But Billy's simple philosophy and blanket honesty, though perhaps offensive or wrongheaded to some, were unencumbered by thoughts of propriety, correctness, or acceptability. In Billy, one got what one saw. I might, in reality, be an ax murderer, but you would not know it until I was upon you. Billy, on the other hand, could not be an ax murderer, because if he was, he would be carrying an ax. In my mind's eye I suddenly envisioned him and Candy straddling his MegaHarley with an adoptive bundle of joy in the sidecar, the three of them tooling briskly down a country road, their faces flush to the wind.

What came out of the adoptive parenting classes were not the dicta I had feared, but a heightened awareness of the range of parental philosophies and responses that exists. Our choosing separate corners of the room after each vignette brought this home in spades. In short, as Carl later made clear, there were no right or wrong answers, just "different" answers. (However, some borders must exist, otherwise the red flag industry would not have a raison d'être.) In fact, after the dynamic on discipline, Carl remarked that the night before his nine-year-old daughter had been a hellion on wheels. "I gave her a whack," he said, swiping the air for emphasis. Billy looked over at me from across the room, as if to say, "On the ass."

The discussions proceeded to parental expectations of the adoptive child, support networks, and the agency's role in postplacement supervision. Then Ann presented a dynamic that made the prospect of adoption more real to me than it had been.

She asked us to close our eyes. A few moments of silence ensued, followed by Ann's quietly reading the following narrative:

You feel yourself being lifted up and carried by someone who smells and feels different. This person even holds you differently. And when the person speaks, the sounds are unfamiliar. You are wrapped in a blanket. A door opens. The wind blows cold against your face. You feel yourself being lowered. There is a slamming sound. A roar. You are moving. After a while you stop. You feel yourself being lifted up again. There is another slamming sound. You are being carried along. There is a lot of noise. Voices. More voices than you have ever heard before. You are carried into a place that smells very strange. The place whistles. Then it roars and you are moving again. Then you and the person holding you are lifted up. It is as if your whole world is being lifted up. And then, after a long, long time, you feel yourself and your world coming down. There is a bump. Once more you are lifted and carried. More slamming and moving and roaring. And then it stops. You are taken into a place where nothing looks familiar. The colors are different. The smell is different. People gather around you. They all touch you. They pass you around. Someone puts food in your mouth, but it is not what you are used to eating. You cry. Someone rocks you. Your eyes close. You are lowered into a bed with a strange feel and smell. The light goes out. You are lying in a dark place and nothing reminds you of anything you have ever known before.

A shudder filled me. Who would my son be? What would it be like to lift him from his friends and caretakers, from the colors and sounds and smells of familiar surroundings? Would he like me? Would he run away when he saw me? Would he get on the plane with me?

In reality, it was too early to dwell on such particulars, for I had not yet even been given the agency's imprimatur to proceed with an adoption. The adoption process is slow and lumbering, with patience being the watchword. But, at some deep level, I knew and the agency knew that we were both anticipating the successful placement of a child at the end of the road. This anticipation would soon become an assumption, which in time would become a certainty.

A theory if you hold it hard enough
And long enough gets rated as a creed.
Robert Frost

On the night of the last session there was a period when we prospective parents were left alone in the room to talk among ourselves. Optimism was running high, although it was seeded with reasonable uncertainties. The middle-America couple wanted an infant. The single woman wanted a group of siblings. Billy and Candy seemed to be open to all the options—instantly heightening them in my estimation. Some of our talk revolved around costs. Oddly enough, though, there was little of the bonding that tends to take place among people who have shared a common, intimate experience. Perhaps this is peculiar to the adoption effort, where the thrust is essentially an individual one: get a child as soon as possible. In short, there is no group goal to be achieved.

Before breaking up, we dutifully exchanged names and addresses. "Let me know as soon as you have your child," was the parting sentiment. But I sensed that there would be no keeping in touch, no alleluia phone calls once the first member of our group had adopted. When we exited the armory and walked outside, I lagged behind a bit, watching as the others pulled away and disappeared into the darkness—exactly the way it should be.

On this last night I had handed over another $1000, plus $10 for the book *Raising Adopted Children*. It was like investing in stocks, I thought, and the dividends were represented by successfully completing each step in the adoption process. The checks had become easier to write too, which reminded me of something I had read in *Anna Karenina* concerning the drinking habit:

"The first one sticks in your throat, the second goes down like a hawk, and the rest are like wee little birds." That first $100 check for the application fee just did not want to leave my hand, but once it had, the $500 check followed in hot pursuit. Now I was beginning to write checks almost reflexively.

I made the long drive home and opened my adoption file folder to check off yet another milestone in the journey toward my faceless child. I had finished my parenting classes.

And I did not have to tell Billy that I loved him.

—— My Turf ——

It began to get real. Now they were going to actually come to my house for a closer look. This was the so-called homestudy.

"It's not a white glove inspection," Carl had assured me as we searched for a date over the phone. Then he laughed before hanging up.

Why did he laugh?

My homestudy was scheduled for August. Perfect: weather warm, skies clear, apples hanging heavy on the branch, Penobscot River coursing serenely behind my house. A picture-perfect place to raise a kid.

I hoped Carl would feel the same. If I had known at the time that he had karaoke on his mind and in his heart, I would not have anticipated his visit with such gravity.

At this point I recapped my status. I had submitted my application, gone through intake, completed parenting classes (I was actually *missing* Billy), and had my physical exam. I had also paid the first three-quarters of my agency fee, and I was not even officially a client of my adoption agency yet. But I was confident of becoming one, having convinced myself that if there had been any

RED FLAGS

they would already have been pointed out to me, thus stopping the process dead in its tracks. So I tried to relax, looking forward to Carl's visit with the composure of someone rooted in a done deal.

Carl arrived just as I was on my hands and knees cleaning the kitchen baseboards with a Q-tip. He came in and remarked on the pleasant appearance of my house.

We sat opposite each other at my kitchen table. The sunlight poured in through the window, falling upon us like a benediction while we sat, quiet as Quakers. Carl had the bearing of someone who knew he had the upper hand—not arrogant, but generously reassuring in a manner that confirmed he was in control of a crucial step in the adoption process. The silence persisted a few moments longer.

Carl hoisted his briefcase onto the table, opened it, and pulled out a file: my autobiography. I had written the eight-page tract as part of my application. Suddenly I wondered if there was anything in there I should be regretting. It covered just about every aspect of my life from birth to the heady anticipation of adoptive parenthood. Carl was now going over it like an attorney scouring a contract for flaws. I tried to remember what I had written and whether any of the evidence would be detrimental to my petition. Or worse yet, did any of the statements constitute a

red flag?

"So, you're *Catholic!*"

Carl had taken me by surprise, and his declaration brought me to attention. I leaned across the table. "Is that good?" I whispered. I remember having written that my Catholic grammar-school experience had been "unhappy."

"*Very* unhappy?" probed Carl as his pen hovered over his legal pad.

"Somewhat unhappy," I countered, bailing water as fast as I could. I was convinced I had not mentioned being put out with the trash in a pitch black incinerator room by my first-grade teacher, Sister Helen Celene, who was eighty-eight at the time and was said to be still alive but no longer teaching. Then I added, "It could have been happier, and in some respects actually was."

Carl scribbled. "Do you intend to raise your son a Catholic?" he asked.

"Yes," I said with a nod. "But a happy Catholic, if not a very happy one."

Carl looked sidelong at me, cracking and then quickly abandoning a weak smile.

We talked about my family. "What do they think about what you're doing?" asked Carl, even though we had gone over this question at intake. He made it sound as if I were harvesting opium in my backyard.

"They're all for it," I said. That was God's truth. I had joined my mother in referring to my prospective son as "Pablo," and this went a long way toward creating a mental picture of what he would look like. "Yes," I confirmed again. "They have no reservations."

"That's remarkable," said Carl.

Well, I didn't think it was remarkable, but perhaps not that common. The books I had read said that families frequently offered some initial resistance to the introduction of an adoptive child, especially one from a foreign bloodline.

The interview progressed through my job description and the prospects for staying employed, the distance of the grammar school from my home, how Pablo would get to and from school, childcare arrangements, my personal support network, medical insurance, the personalities of my neighbors, the likelihood of a meteoric impact on my home. Whew! I felt as if I were being peeled. I wished Carl would just ask me if I were a good witch or a bad witch and get it over with.

At that point a friend came by, and not a moment too soon. Mary had written one of the three reference letters that had been submitted with my application. Part of the process required that one of these people be personally interviewed in my absence, so it was necessary for me to step outside. As Mary sat down for her cross-examination, she laid a platter of freshly baked sticky buns before Carl.

Good girl, Mary!

I sat outside on my back porch for the longest time, watching the river curl south in long silver ribbons. Goldfinches came to the feeder from their haven in the immense silver maples growing along the bank. Raspberries were swelling on their canes. The sky was bluer than Seattle's. God, I thought, all of this is being squandered on one person. I need to share it with someone, preferably a little black-haired boy from Latin America.

A dangerous line of thought had been snaking its way into my head for some weeks now. I had tried to dislodge it for my own emotional well-being. But I now had to acknowledge its permanence: I was assuming the adoption of a child. When I looked at the raspberries, Pablo was picking them; when I walked along the river bank, he was there with me, his small hand in mine; when I cooked a meal, I imagined calling a little boy to the table and feigning annoyance when he showed reluctance to abandon his play. "It's happened," I whispered. What on earth will I do if all this doesn't work out? What on earth will I do?

At the end of an hour and a half Mary emerged—smiling. She came through the screen door. "It's okay," she said, as if the fix was in.

When I went back into the house Carl was licking his fingers. A few sticky buns remained on the platter. "Good woman," he said after swallowing. "And a good friend."

"And a good cook," I chided as Carl made a last few smacking sounds.

Carl smiled. "Now," he said. "What kind of child were we talking about at intake?"

Everything really *was* okay, then. I was being asked to paint my child's portrait. "Young, school aged," I said, resuming my seat. "Four to six."

"Why not a baby?" asked Carl as he reached for another sticky bun.

"What would I do with a baby?" I asked. "It never occurred to me to even consider it. Anyway, how would a single man take care of an infant?"

"It's been done," said Carl.

"How would I afford the childcare?"

"That's something to consider."

"And I think an infant needs a mother."

Carl scribbled. "Are we talking about a boy, then?"

"Of course." But he already knew that. Why were we going over trodden ground? Perhaps they wanted me to repeat myself to assure them that I knew what I wanted. Or maybe Carl was simply forgetful.

"Why?"

I had thought a lot about this one. "Carl, I don't think I could be a role model for a girl. Besides, isn't it going to be hard enough for me, as a single man, to adopt a boy?"

Carl scribbled with one hand while he reached for a sticky bun with the other. "What about nationality?" he asked.

"Hispanic," I said. "Didn't I tell you that at intake?" I recognized the edge of annoyance in my voice, but felt that, having come this far, I could afford to assert myself a bit.

"Yes, but you gave no justification."

"I speak Spanish, and since a school-aged kid is very verbal it seemed like an advantage to be able to talk to him."

Carl put down a few last words, clicked his pen, and pocketed it. "Can I see the house?"

We went from corner to corner of my small clapboard home, winding up in Pablo's room. "Nice," said Carl. As I stood on the threshold looking in, the room seemed pregnant with possibility. I swelled with anticipation. I had built all the furniture in it. On the low bed was a superheroes comforter. Dinosaur curtains hung across the windows. Suddenly a small sleeping boy appeared in my mind's eye. I could see the rise and fall of his chest. I could hear his subtle exhalations. Then it struck me: This child is already alive, in a place as different from Maine as can be; he is absolutely unaware of me, and yet I have somehow invoked his spirit by putting these charms in place.

Carl packed up his papers. He eyed the last of the sticky buns and in the next moment had seized it. I saw him to the back porch.

"I'll submit this and then you'll get a call to come down to the office to read it."

"Lewiston?"

"Yes."

"I'll book passage on the packet."

"Hmmm?"

"Good-bye, Carl."

Once Carl was safely on his way I felt the most incredible compulsion to ascend the stairs to Pablo's room. I lingered on the threshold for a moment, gazing in, as if awaiting his invitation to enter. I sat down on the edge of his bed and stroked the comforter, my hand passing over the triumphant faces of Superman and Wonder Woman. I turned my head to the window and watched the river roll south, south, always south, the sun blinking off its surface, the pendulous branches of the silver maples sweeping the bank.

God, what a wonderful place to raise a child.

Red at Last

In this age of electronic mail and the fax, I have no idea why I had to drive to Lewiston to read my homestudy. The invitation to do so came in a call from Ann, the woman who had assisted Carl at the parenting classes. I felt that another giant step had been completed. I was being asked to read the homestudy because it was worth reading. Did this mean I had passed?

It was November, three months since the home visit and eight months since I had submitted my application. Carl was now history. One early autumn evening he left a message on my answering machine. "But I'll be interested in seeing what kind of kid you wind up with" were his closing words.

As I drove the interminable miles to Lewiston, my breath was constantly being taken away by the autumn landscape bordering Interstate 95. When the soothing greens of August give way to the shocking golds of October, I become hypersensitive about the passage of time. That autumn, the passage was particularly unnerving, making me feel anxious about my plans for a son, as if the ball were rolling much too fast, as if my son's arrival were imminent and then what on earth would I do? At other times, my heightened sense of time endowed me with a feeling that things were happening too slowly and that I wanted the adoption now, at this very moment.

When I got to the armory the doors were locked. I was ten minutes early. I took out my copy of *Raising Adopted Children* and sat on a park bench facing the building. There were several young teens carousing on its granite steps. They were tormenting one another, the boys against the girls. The girls wanted the boys' attention, but they were pretending that the girls did not exist. This led to occasional screaming and feigned hitting. The activity was monotonous and went on without letup. I was sure it would last the night. Then, for only a moment, I imagined my son as a teenager, wondering what the autumn evenings of his fourteenth year would be like.

Ann arrived. She came over to the bench and then we both headed for the door, wading through the kids. They parted for us in such an incidental way that it did not interrupt their horseplay. Ann seemed apologetic. "Have you ever imagined your son as a teen?"

"Not until now," I said. Ann's expression solicited clarification, but I had none to give, so we continued into the office.

I sat down at a round table and Ann pulled out my homestudy. She left me alone while I read it through. Almost immediately I began to pick up inconsistencies, misleading statements, and inaccurate information. I recalled having mentioned to Carl during the home visit that my grammar-school experience had not been the best. On paper he made it sound as if the nuns had locked me in a closet with rats. When I had spoken matter-of-factly about the ethnic and racial diversity of the New Jersey neighborhood where I grew up, Carl had, with the best of intentions no doubt, inserted commentary that made me look too good to be true. "Robert has no prejudices and is accepting of all peoples, religions, and cultures." I realized that as my advocate the agency had to make me look presentable, but I was leery about risking comparison with Albert Schweitzer. I dutifully noted every passage that gave me trouble, grammatically, stylistically, or contentwise, and handed it over to Ann. "It's not bad," I said, "but these corrections will make it more accurate."

"I haven't read the homestudy myself," she said, "but I'll pass on your comments to your caseworker."

She had not read the homestudy? I wondered if I should point out the red flags I saw in the *agency's* operation. But I was preempted by Ann, who raised an index finger and said, "There is a small problem, though."

I caught my breath. A problem? But I'm the one who is accepting of all peoples, religions, and cultures!

"It's something that came up at the parenting class," she continued. "We didn't want to point it out then, thinking it better to discuss it in private."

I found myself frozen in my seat, my eyes begging for clarification. I tried to recall everything I had said at those meetings, wondering why Billy wasn't sitting in the hot seat instead of me.

"Do you have any idea what it could be?" Ann asked.

I thought hard. Was it my questioning the agency's fee? Did that indicate lack of financial wherewithal? Was it my reluctance to consider adopting an infant? Had I offended someone by playing "Wipeout" behind my head on a toy guitar during one of our breaks?

"No," I said. "I have no idea."

Ann's response was anticlimactic. "Do you remember the question we asked you folks about whether you tend to get attached quickly to people or whether it takes you a long time to warm to someone?"

My eyes shifted rapidly back and forth as I took in all of this. "Yes," I said. "I remember."

"What was your response?"

Was I on the witness stand or something? What should I say? What could I say?

"I get quickly attached," I offered, my mouth closing quickly about the last word, as if I could inhale the whole statement should it prove to be the wrong answer.

"Right," said Ann in the manner of a kindergarten teacher. Only she did not add "Very good."

"Is this a problem?" I asked, leaning forward.

"We need to discuss this," she said.

I swallowed hard for both of us. "It's not," I began. "It's not a red flag, is it?"

Ann brought her thumb and index finger together, offering a faint smile. "A small one."

I recalled the small green flags that we as kids would wave at the St. Patrick's Day parade. Small, yes, but without them, no free hot dogs from the Irish vendors, no membership in the club. "But why?" I asked.

Ann smiled again, benignly, as if my unfamiliarity with the tenets of social work struck her as quaint. "What we're afraid of is that you'll get quickly attached to your child and will feel hurt if he does not immediately return your affection."

I felt as if I were floating in some thick liquid. My senses seemed dulled and I had trouble thinking. I repeated, "Is this a problem?"

Ann nodded, still smiling. "We just want you to remain aware of your tendency, so you won't set yourself up for disappointment."

I was stuck on the word *tendency.* How could a tendency be distilled from a single, forgettable (though not to Ann) statement? I realized that I could just as easily have said that it takes a long time for me to warm to someone. And what about Billy, damn it?

"I am so apprised," I said, contritely, seeking the path of least resistance, although the coals were still flaming within.

At this point, I remember thinking that adoption agency personnel do not seem to dwell in the same world as their clients. It is as if they were born and bred within the walls of their agencies. But I know this not to be true; many of these people have multiple adopted children of their own. So where did the gravity of some of their interpretations come from—a need to show that they have read the right books? I still have no answer to this, but with all the adopted children and families experiencing real crises, indulging in polemics seemed like a trivial pursuit.

"Your caseworker will be Laura," said Ann as she put her papers away. "She'll help you choose a program."

A program, a country from which to adopt. I gathered this prospect under my skin and left the armory, passing between the teens who were still going at each other. This time they fell silent when I approached, like crickets.

I stopped at a Wendy's on the way home. It was just before closing. The salad bar was still illuminated. "It's on the house," said an employee as he passed by with mop in hand. "We have to throw it out anyway."

I rubbed my chin, hovering over the broccoli crock. The vegetable was dark and wilted, soft looking. I thought to myself, "It is good that the broccoli looks so terrible, lest I should grow too fond of it." Then I stepped up to the counter and ordered a cheeseburger.

The Labyrinth

From the very beginning, I had intuitively sensed that at some point things would get difficult. But I did not think it would be so soon.

After reading my homestudy in Lewiston, it was the longest time before someone from the agency called me. I lapsed into a sense that I was not really involved in the adoption process at all and that if I did not mention the subject again no one else would either.

To maintain the illusion of momentum, I began an aggressive reading program, buying books and perusing magazine articles relevant to the adoption subculture. Many of the pieces related either alleluia stories or tales of incredible frustration, despair, and scandal. In the interest of culling as much affirmation and encouragement as possible, I soon learned to feed almost exclusively on the success stories. I also found out about an organization called the Committee for Single Adoptive Parents, which published a "source list" of agencies that had worked successfully with singles. When I received the list my heart quickened. But on closer reading my spirits sank. I saw NO MEN highlighted at the tail end of most of the program descriptions. Still, there were enough agencies that would work with men to encourage me to persist.

My caseworker finally called and introduced herself. She sounded pleasant, with a grandmotherly quaver in her voice that bespoke experience and had a quality of "All will be well and all is well." At this point it had been eight months since my initial application. To me, Laura's call represented some truly concrete movement in the direction of a flesh-and-blood child. Laura said she was sending me form I-600A, "Application for Advance Processing of Orphan Petition." I would need to take this to an office of the Immigration and Naturalization Service to pave the way for my prospective son's visa to enter the United States. She was also sending me some information on specific programs.

I waited with bated breath for the I-600A, which arrived two days later. I filled out the form on my lunch break and sprinted over to the INS office in Bangor. I was fingerprinted there and told that processing the application would take about forty-five days. The fee for this service was $140—nonrefundable if the petition was denied.

The next day Laura's program information arrived. I felt that I could not read the packets fast enough to satisfy myself, as if there were only a few kids left in the world to adopt and if I did not act immediately they would be taken by somebody else.

The packets were from two different agencies, Thursday's Child in Connecticut and Rainbow House in New Mexico (at this point my home agency had no foreign programs of its own that were suitable for me.) The Thursday's Child agency was promoting Peruvian adoptions, whereas Rainbow House dealt with Albania and Russia.

Albania?

I read the Albanian program description first out of pure curiosity:

> Travel to and out of Albania has been banned for nearly 48 years. As such, diseases common to other European countries, such as AIDS and hepatitis B, have not yet been identified in Albania. Our Albanian coordinator will ask for the children to be seen by a local pediatrician and will attempt to have children medically evaluated and possibly tested for AIDS. However, Rainbow House cannot assure the veracity or accuracy of any tests, evaluations, or results obtained on children or be held liable for medical reports or social and physical assessments of the children.

Was I ready for this degree of uncertainty about my prospective child?

I skipped over to the Russian program description. It seemed less adventurous than the Albania gambit: "We have a good working relationship with the Russian adoption authorities and the children available to us appear to be well cared for."

Neither the Albanian nor the Russian program information said anything about singles. "Family" was the operative word. The Peruvian program, however, stated the acceptability of singles right up front, but it also sounded like a yard sale. "Single men and women and couples, at least 18 years older than child. No upper age limit.... More babies, some toddlers, and some older children. Range of skin color from light tan to brown."

Peru certainly seemed democratic as far as the nature of its adoptive parents was concerned. It was also in line with my plans to adopt a Hispanic child. I called Laura and indicated my interest.

"Yes, Peru will let anyone adopt," she said, unflatteringly.

"Is that good?"

"Well, we don't know where these kids come from. There are stories that these are hardened street kids who are rounded up for foreign adoption. Some of them may even have parents."

"Are you telling me not to adopt from Peru?"

"No. I'm just saying that you should be careful."

"But what do you mean? How should I be careful? If you help me to adopt from Peru, is that being careful?"

The discussion went in circles from there, but further deliberations regarding Peru were obviated when, several days later, political upheaval caused the country to close its ports.

I retreated to my notes from the initial orientation session in Lewiston. I kept getting caught up on either the phenomenal fees for some of the Latin American countries or the unwillingness of these programs to deal with single men. I felt a little panicky now. If it were to succeed at all, I needed to sense that the process was always moving forward, if only at a crawl. I felt that my agency had not yet given me anything solid to go on. What I wanted it to say was, "Here's an orphanage in Country X. They have a lot of kids in the age group you're looking for. Let's try this."

But instead there was just a stretch of dead air. I once again heard nothing from my agency, which impelled me to take up the search on my own. I continued to go down the list from the orientation, firming my lips and shaking my head as I read the program descriptions for the different countries—either too expensive or not open to single men.

Then, an echo of something that had been said at that meeting: American Catholics of Polish ancestry have an advantage in adopting from Poland. That is what Janet had said. Suddenly it seemed somehow right. I called Laura and shared my feelings. Her response: "Let's go for it."

I immediately began to make inquiries on every front. I wrote letters to all the agencies in the country that dealt with Polish adoptions, and waited for their replies. An independent facilitator working in Connecticut was curt: "Children should have two parents." Several of the agencies were bamboozled by my inquiry: They simply did not know if Poland would allow single adoptions. "We've never tried it," read one reply. Nor, apparently, were they willing to.

I was surprised, but delighted, to receive a call from Hope Marindin, the director of the Committee for Single Adoptive Parents, to whom I had also written. She had spoken, on my behalf, to Anna Johnson, the woman in charge of the Polish program at an agency in Massachusetts called Wide Horizons for Children. "Send Anna a photo of yourself and a copy of your homestudy," Hope said. "She leaves for Poland next week."

My spirits soared. I thought to myself, "She's leaving for Poland and will take my picture and homestudy with her!" In my mind this translated into more than possibility. It was tacit approval. I immediately called Laura, whose enthusiasm seemed wired to my own. "What a coincidence!" she cackled. "I know Anna Johnson and am meeting with her today!"

All will be well and all is well.

Overnight Pablo's room had become Stash's room. I called my parents and told them of the change in plans. They were heartily supportive, perhaps feeling that adopting a child in the Polish bloodline (my ancestry is predominantly Polish) was in some oblique way closer to natural childbirth than what I had previously planned.

On my way to work the next day, I went to the library and took out Michener's *Poland* to get a panoramic cross-section of the country's history and culture in one megadose. That evening, while at dinner with friends, another coincidence arose: Don, a contractor, was doing work for a Polish emigré woman not far from Bangor. My eyebrows took flight. A sign! "Do you think she'd give me Polish lessons?"

A week later, while Anna Johnson was still in Poland, I found myself sitting at the kitchen table of a madwoman. Her name was Jadwiga Smentkowski. About sixty-five, with weathered blond hair and powder visibly lying in the cracks of her careworn face, she taught Polish with a vengeance—for $10 an hour. The frenzied lessons were punctuated with tales of her woes extending back across the sea to a city called Bydgoszcz (which I mispronounced "By Gosh"). She would retrieve herself from these digressions with a fury, making up for lost time by pounding on the table, forcing me to attack the cryptic pronunciation of the impossibly consonated Polish language.

"I can't," I finally said halfway through that first lesson. "I just can't!" I lowered my head onto the table but jerked it heavenward when Jadwiga's fist came down hard right next to my ear. "The days of the week!" she commanded. I complied, repeating them in Polish until, like a song, they became stuck in my brain, if only for the time being.

As I drove home after that first lesson, I kept reminding myself of the noble cause for which I was enduring the Beast of By Gosh. Then I would lapse into self-recrimination for being so impetuous in leaping into Polish. A week later Laura called. Anna Johnson had returned from Poland. "The people she spoke with will not consider an adoption by a single."

My disappointment was tempered by the realization that I would not have to return for a second Polish lesson. But hope for a Polish adoption flared anew when I received a call the next evening from a woman lawyer in Connecticut. Her name was Maria Tomaszewski. An agency to which I had written had passed on my letter to her. She was a facilitator for Polish adoptions and was on her way to Poland. She expressed optimism. "They've allowed single women to adopt," she reasoned. "I don't see why they should discriminate against men. In any case, I'll advocate for you and will call you when I get back at the end of the month."

I was now convinced that the Polish adoption would work. Not only were people acting on my behalf, but I felt that by reading about Poland and taking Polish lessons I was anointing my efforts with a positive energy that would make things happen in my favor. A few days later I was back at Jadwiga's kitchen table, enduring the drumbeat of her fist against the formica as she oscillated between present-tense declensions and lament for a lost love in Warsaw named Ignacz. Sometimes her frenzy was such that spit flew from her mouth as foaming emboli. But I persisted, and I found that I was, indeed, learning Polish. It was all due to Jadwiga's highly pressured way of teaching: When I did really badly she would strike me on the arm, but when I did well she would give me sponge cake.

It was now January 1992, and I had been pursuing an adoption for ten months. All I had to show for my time and anxiety was the uncertain hope that I would soon be winging my way to Warsaw, of all places. I focused on the end of the month with the faith and anticipation of a zealot, awaiting the promised call from Maria Tomaszewski, the call that would tell me there was a certain five year old named Stanislaw, his nose pressed up against the cold pane of an orphanage, waiting for his family. Such visions helped me to embrace my Polish lessons with an intensity that brought Jadwiga, in a moment of lucidity, to take my hand in hers and call me "gifted."

And then came the great disillusionment.

A very cold January passed unceremoniously into a very cold February, but Maria's promised call did not materialize. On the first day of the new month I called her, but there was no answer. Day after day I continued to call to no avail. By the end of February it was time to give up. All of my other letters regarding Polish adoptions had either gone unanswered or offered little hope of success. When I told Jadwiga I was discontinuing my Polish lessons, she pressed the back of her hand to her head and threw herself onto the sofa, wanting only a dagger. She really did not need one, for I had already pierced her heart.

I called Laura and told her I was abandoning the Polish option. Her attitude was one of understanding, and then she offered something of her own. My agency in Lewiston had started a Russian program, and although currently they were dealing only with married couples, there was some indication that the Russians might consider singles on a case-by-case basis. I would have to talk with the agency's new director, a woman named Kerry, who was personally facilitating the new program. I told Laura that I was interested.

So it was Russia now. Not Stanislaw after all, but Pavel.

In early March Kerry called me. She sounded young and harried. Kerry repeated what Laura had told me: a slim chance of success, depending on whether the Russian adoption authorities felt comfortable with me. Three days later I had the application in hand. I was also told to, as quickly as possible, put together my "family album"—a set of photographs detailing my life and describing my home environment.

In the middle of March Laura called. "I have two children sitting right here on my desk," she said, meaning she had photographs.

"Actual kids?" I pleaded.

"Yes. I think one is perfect for you. His name is Sasha, and he has a mop of blond hair and the cutest little nose."

I was barely able to speak. Was she telling me that all I had to do was say *da* and Sasha was mine? If so, the answer was *Da! Da!*

"I'll tag him for you," said Laura. "We've received your application and Kerry will give you a call tomorrow to discuss details."

Details. Details of what? Of my trip to Russia? I was too awash in images, hopes, and expectations to even think straight. I hung up without asking the questions that would occur to me in afterthought. I wanted to be in control of events, but I had learned that in adoption the client has the least control of all, like a man trying to climb a greased flagpole. From Peru to Poland to Russia, I felt as if I had been blown first here and then there by powerful winds. All that I could do was gather my coat more tightly about myself and blink dumbly.

Kerry called the next day, as promised. I wanted her to tell me that Sasha was well and tickled to hear about the imminent arrival of his new dad. But her tone was businesslike. "We've consulted our sovietologist about your case."

Their "sovietologist"? They had a sovietologist?

She continued, "With all the couples wanting to adopt from Russia, our sovietologist feels that your chances of success as a single are poor."

I suddenly felt my son, my Sasha, falling away from me. "But I thought you said I would be considered on an individual basis," I argued. "You were the one who suggested I try Russia."

Kerry relented a tad. "I still think you should try," she said. "I just don't want to get your hopes up."

"Hope is all I have left."

I listened as Kerry sighed. "Well, we can try the Russians. I'll need a thousand dollars from you to start the ball rolling."

We hung up. Was I doing the right thing now? If a Russian adoption was all but impossible, why was I pursuing it? To show how much I could take?

The next day I sent Kerry $1000. The day after that I sent in my family album. In late March Judy the sovietologist left for Moscow.

It had now been one year since my initial orientation.

For days after my telephone confrontation with Kerry I felt worked up. I feared a Russian adoption would fail. But even the attempt was *something,* and I desperately needed to know that something was happening. I also needed someone to talk to, but who among my friends would understand the arcana of the adoption underworld? Who would or could care enough to offer advice rooted in experience? But I didn't want advice. At this point I just wanted to be comforted.

I returned to my agency listings, picking through them like Fagin with his baubles. The names of these places bespoke opportunity, if anything: Adoptions Unlimited, Casa del Mundo, Wide Horizons, Rainbow House. But I saw nothing that was likely to work for me.

I called Laura, just to talk. I wanted consolation and yet I feared appearing weak. Perhaps this was all part of the deal. If I lasted more than a year, my fortunes would turn because I would be deemed tough enough to follow through on an adoption. But my despondency made its way through the façade of confidence I was struggling to generate. "Do you want to quit?" Laura asked.

I was astonished by the question. Yet, at some level, I realized that it had to be asked. "No," I said, quietly. "For the first time in my adult life I really know my own mind. If this is as hard and frustrating as it gets, then I think I can take it."

"It may get worse," said Laura.

For the rest of March and into April I tried to turn my attentions to affairs other than adoption — my work, a long-overdue oil change, reading short fiction. But a call from Kerry in mid-April yanked me back onto center stage like the muscular arm of a hanging judge. "Judy's back from Russia," she announced.

I was already begging. "And? And? . . ."

"The Russians won't hear of it," she said. "Sorry."

"What about Sasha?" I persisted, without hope.

"Who's he?"

I explained that Laura had tagged him as a possibility for me.

"Oh," said Kerry. "We've found a family for him."

I would not have thought it possible to become so angry so quickly. "When?" I demanded. "With whom?" This was only part of what was boiling within. Kerry said that she had found a "family." So what did that make me, an alien entity?

"How about a fourteen-year-old Dominican boy?" she offered, taking no note of my emotional state. "Or a Guatemalan infant?"

What was this, a grab bag? Where were these kids coming from?

"Kerry!" I said. "I'm not looking for a teenager or a baby. And if you've read my homestudy you know I haven't been approved for these age groups."

Silence.

The truth was, I now felt that my agency was taking an attitude of "We know what's best for you." The only way to satisfy them seemed to be to throw myself at their mercy and take whatever child they could come up with. But I had no interest in satisfying them. I wanted to satisfy myself. I wanted some control back. I wanted the flagpole to be degreased.

The line remained quiet for some time, during which I roused the mantra that edged me back toward center: "I am the consumer... I am the consumer... I am the consumer...." My outrage slowly subsided.

"I'm sure Laura will be in touch with you soon," said Kerry.

"Okay," I answered, softly, with nothing more to say. Then we hung up.

Both Napoleon and Hitler had failed in Russia. The futility of my own efforts with that country should have been evident from the start. Once again there was the odd relief of at least knowing that a particular door was closed to me. I did not have to waste time figuring out how to open it. I started to think about myself again, instead of some unknown child I imagined to be waiting for me in some far-flung region of the world. I began by acknowledging the fact that I was hungry. That evening I went to a Chinese restaurant and ordered cashew chicken. However, I was barred from any enjoyment of the food by the realization that I was trying to manhandle emotions that wanted to have their say. At the end of the meal I received my fortune cookie. The slip seemed to have been deliberately planted:

HAPPY EVENTS WILL TAKE PLACE SHORTLY IN YOUR HOME

Fuga del Diavolo

Like a wrestler tossed out of the ring, I crawled back onto the mat to see how much more I could take from a seemingly invulnerable opponent. My spirits buoyed somewhat when my agency returned my $1000 from the failed Russian gambit. At first they had wanted to refund only $800, but I agitated for the full sum: It was emotionally difficult to be failing at adoption, but I had no intention of paying for the privilege.

Laura called. She tossed a name out to me—Dave Penn. He sat on the agency's advisory board and had adopted two children from Guatemala. "He's interested in promoting Guatemalan adoptions," Laura told me, suggesting he might have some special connections I could access. "Give him a call."

I had nothing to lose.

When I called, his twelve-year-old son answered the phone, sounding anything but Latino. He had the distracted tone of a teenager who would rather be elsewhere. He screamed for his father.

Dave was a banker, but he sounded like any other Mainer, which means he could just as easily have been a potato farmer or a school bus driver. I told him what my situation was. "Can you help me?" I asked, perhaps expecting that he would immediately perform some miracle.

Dave was sympathetic, but the ostensible "special connections" Laura had told me about were not in evidence. Dave was married and therefore had had no problem with his adoptions. It soon became apparent to me that he, like almost everyone else, did not quite know what to make of me. "I went through Wide Horizons for Children in Massachusetts," he told me. "I can call them on your behalf if you'd like."

What could I say? I could call them on my own behalf. Then I could answer their questions directly. But this seemed to be the only thing Dave was able to offer me at the moment, and I have a debilitating tendency to be kind, so I murmured my assent.

We continued to become acquainted over the phone, but the conversation floundered. Then Dave spoke up animatedly, struck by a thought. "I could call the orphanage I work with in Guatemala," he offered. "Then we could know immediately whether it's worth it to proceed through an agency here."

Now this was concrete information I could use. I had learned through my readings of the source listings of the Committee for Single Adoptive Parents that just because an agency is willing to work with single men (most were) was no indication that specific foreign provinces or orphanages they dealt with would (most would not). I asked Dave to go ahead and do what he could for me.

Earlier I had begun subscribing to a photolisting service of the International Concerns Committee for Children in Denver. The ICCC is a clearinghouse for children from all over the world in need of families. Various agencies and groups (like Americans for African Adoptions) around the country send photos and information to the ICCC to be reproduced and mailed out to subscribers looking for adoptable children. Most of the kids were the hardest of the hard-luck stories: street children, refugees, and those with horrendous birth defects. There were also a lot of sibling groups, most of which were not to be broken up—it was the thirteen-year-old Gypsy girl and her three little brothers or nothing at all. For an annual $25 fee I received hefty monthly mailings, which I filed in a ring binder supplied by the ICCC. It was heartbreaking reading. These were the rejectees. Yet by the next mailing many of them would have been adopted by caring souls somewhere in the United States or Canada.

Shortly after my conversation with Dave, I received my third or fourth ICCC mailing. I settled into my desk chair, turned on the overhead lamp, and began my languid turning of the pages.

"Suk Wu is two. He is blind and missing all of his toes, but he loves to smile and has a good appetite."

"Juanito was found in a dumpster in São Paulo but is no worse for wear because of this experience! He has a severe cleft palate which is partially operable."

"Luz, Jaime, and Enrique are siblings. All were physically and sexually abused by their father. . . ."

Halfway through the files my eye settled on a little Honduran boy with light hair and crossed eyes named Roberto. He seemed to be clapping. I dog-eared the page and continued to leaf through the binder. When I had finished I came back to Roberto: three-and-a-half, no parents, well cared for in an orphanage in Tegulcigalpa. Then, at the tail end of the listing, an annotation: singles accepted.

Would it be foolish to race to the phone and offer to adopt this kid? Would appearing too eager be construed as a

red flag?

I waited out the night, all the while knowing that first thing in the morning I would call the agency handling this child and sound just as anxious to adopt as I did now.

The agency was in New Jersey: Casa del Mundo. I called at a respectable midmorning hour and found myself speaking with the director. She sounded elated to hear from me, as if she had been expecting my call. It made me feel good. I mentioned the ICCC photolisting of Roberto and in a focused, nonhysterical way indicated my interest. I felt slightly strange about it all, this shopping for a child over the phone. I could have been anybody. Hell, I *was* anybody, yet this woman was treating me like a tried-and-true client. As such, she was up front: "Roberto is long gone. But he was a cutie, wasn't he?"

I did not feel too significant a letdown because I had not invested all that much of myself in little Roberto. In short, I was learning—learning how to protect myself.

The director of Casa del Mundo did not want to let me go, though. "What age group have you been approved for?" she asked. I told her four to six years. "You'll have no problem," she said. "The demand for older kids is very shallow. Especially boys. I can't believe you've been having a problem."

Now I poured out a portion of my heart. I was having problems, indeed. "It's not so much the agencies here in the States," she assured me. "It's the orphanage or region of the foreign country you're dealing with," she said, confirming my own conclusions. "I wish I had a kid to offer you at the moment."

We parted amicably. The demand for these kids was "shallow," yet she could not help me? It was a paradox. The whole business was paradoxical: hundreds of thousands of kids in need of homes, yet all of them were seemingly beyond my reach.

I realized I now had to toss my net a little wider and let other people know of my intention to adopt. That night I drove down to the coast to visit some friends, Maria, a Colombian, and her husband Alejandro, from Argentina. South Americans are the best commiserators in the world. I relished being with them, especially in my time of need. When I told Maria, she was ecstatic . . . at first. But then, on second thought, "Oh, Roberto, why do you want to complicate your life?"

I ducked the red herring. "Can you help me?" I asked, knowing Maria to be a woman wild with connections throughout South America.

I had flattered her and she sprang into action. "I have a cousin in Miami named Patricia. (She's single. Are you interested? She'll be here for Christmas!) Her aunt is the director of an orphanage in my home city of Medellín called La Casita de Nicolás."

I watched in amazement as Maria ran to the phone, raised her cousin, and then poured a river of Spanish into the line. "Okay!" she finally said, hanging up. Then she returned to me. "She'll call! She's very optimistic. And besides, it will cost you only two hundred dollars in Colombia, although you'll have to pay airfare as well. But don't worry!"

How could I worry? Maria was infectious, and at $200 I began to wonder why all the other fees I had been quoted were so hefty. I had raised this question with Laura at one point, and although she seemed uncertain of her facts, she suggested that much of the money went to the orphanage to support children who would never be adopted. This consideration went a long way toward mollifying me and my checkbook.

I left Maria and Alejandro's with feelings of quiet contentment and affective warmth, as when someone else's child falls asleep against my shoulder on a bus. But I did not want to *depend* on them. I still needed to feel that I was doing something under my own steam, that I had other irons in the fire, that I was still creating that aura of positive energy that would bring an adoption to fruition. As such, I returned to my source list from the Committee for Single Adoptive Parents. I found two agencies with similar names: Adoption Unlimited and Adoption*s* Unlimited, the former in Pennsylvania and the latter in California. Adoption Unlimited was facilitating adoptions in Costa Rica, Adoptions Unlimited in Mexico. Both listed no proscriptions against male applicants. When I spoke with the women directors at each agency (adoption facilitation is an overwhelmingly female field), they were both happy to hear from me and offered to help. Maria in California said she would call Mexico, her home country, and Mary in Pennsylvania said she would call Costa Rica. I found Mary to be so empathetic, straight talking, and knowledgeable that I was unmanned to the point of giving her my calling card number, with no fear of seeing a phone bill for $2000 in a month's time.

Suddenly I felt that I was really smoking. I had four people out there slugging for me while I paced in the dugout, sucking on a wad of anxiety-brand tobacco. Dave was on the line with Guatemala and Massachusetts, Maria with Colombia, the other Maria with Mexico, and Mary with Costa Rica.

¡Caramba!

It was a propitious start to the month of May.

I had now been involved in the adoption process for fourteen months. Once again the belief swelled within me that no one who was working at adoption as hard as I could fail. I still believed that my agency should be doing the advocating for me. That is what I was paying it for. Yet I was reluctant to raise this issue with them in any forceful way for fear they might make things difficult for me by intent, rather than by the neglect to which I was becoming accustomed.

I felt strong by the middle of May. As I seeded my lettuce and radishes I considered what might be germinating for me in the adoption arena. Every time the phone rang my heart caught in my throat. Every mail delivery saw me meeting the letter carrier halfway up the drive. One day he remarked, "Nothing important, just advertising." I was grimly annoyed at his preempting my anticipation of the mail.

Before long, the lettuce and radishes broke through the ground, the days became intoxicatingly warm and fresh with the smell of grass cuttings, and the yellow dust of pine pollen covered my windshield. Then, one day, the phone rang. Over the course of the ensuing week it rang three more times.

Dave's orphanage would not consider a single man. His agency in Massachusetts was unable to help.

Maria was distraught. Medellín would not deal with a single man. "How could they be so *stupid!*" she lamented, and then, collecting herself, "You still want to meet my cousin Patricia, don't you?"

Maria from Adoptions Unlimited could get no response from Mexico. She suggested Hungary (!) at $20,000 (!), excluding airfare.

Mary Murphy said Costa Rica would not allow a single man to adopt. "But you'll be successful. I want you to promise to send me a picture of you and your son."

"My son." I had never spoken those words aloud, and I now felt that I probably never would. I became filled with the most incredible desperation.

Laura was right. It had gotten much worse.

In the Land of the Maya

Fourteen months . . . I had been involved in the adoption process for fourteen months and all I had to show for it was a completed homestudy and mounting expenses, not to mention emotional wear and tear. I recalled what Janet had said about the time frame from application to referral of a child: "A child will normally be referred within a year of application." I was overdue.

After my failures with Colombia, Mexico, Costa Rica, and Guatemala, as well as Russia and Poland, I literally did not know where to turn. On the one hand I found myself angry with my agency for being so quiescent; yet, on an intellectual level, I recognized that perhaps a period of emotional reorganization was needed before I could press the effort anew.

A respite was not to be. I had stirred the pot on so many fronts that tidbits began to surface again. A friend at work, an adoptive parent himself, routed a package to me that had crossed his desk. It was from an organization called Guatemala's Children based in California. It was not an agency, but rather a private adoption source. The woman who ran it single-handedly worked with a facilitator in Guatemala City who located adoptable children for Americans. I felt immediately hesitant about putting my faith in a nonagency adoption operation, especially because many of the scandals I had read about had taken place in California. Still, the information might come in handy at some point, so I made a copy of the package and filed it away.

Then a letter arrived from the executive director of the Committee for Single Adoptive Parents. She had not relinquished interest in my case, and, God bless her heart, she was still angling around in the Polish arena for me. The bottom line was that although single women had adopted from Poland, usually with difficulty, the picture was grim for single men. I was not disheartened by this information because I felt that I already knew more than most people about the bleak possibilities for me in Poland. Her advice seemed moot, but I did gain strength from her closing paragraph: "You have going for you . . . the fact that both adoptive couples and single women overwhelmingly do not want to adopt boys, so boys of almost every age are always in surplus."

Surplus — like army jeeps and government cheese. I pictured these boys warehoused and waiting.

The phone rang. It was Laura. "How's it going?" she asked. The note of sympathy in her voice was profound.

"Laura," I said, "I just don't know where it's going, if it's going at all."

After a few words of affirmation, Laura mentioned yet another possibility. "Kerry has started, or rather rejuvenated, a Guatemalan program that used to be very active here."

Guatemala yet again. This was the third time it was knocking. "Go on."

"We have a contact on the east coast of the country. You have to go through the jungle to get there. If you decide to go for it, I'm tempted to go with you."

The jungles of Guatemala. It sounded exotic and immediately captured my imagination. "What's involved in this program?" I asked.

Laura hesitated. "Well, it's not really a set program. We're not even sure if it will work for you. But we do have this contact there and Kerry asked if you wanted her to pursue it."

"I need to think about it, Laura. After the Russian debacle, I'm hesitant about working with Kerry again. I mean, I almost lost money dealing with her."

Then Laura confided something that disturbed me deeply. "Bob," she said, "unless you had given them that thousand dollars they wouldn't even have made inquiries on your behalf."

I became angry. I could not believe that my home agency was not even willing to ask the Russians to consider my application without money in hand. Especially when out-of-state agencies who did not even know me considered this to be part of their service, going out of their way to seek out possibilities for me. "Laura," I said, "I am angrier now than I have ever been."

Laura spoke at length with me regarding her own feelings about how things were going. "You know," she said, "I'm supposed to be retiring from the agency to pursue my own interests."

"Don't leave me now, Laura," I begged.

"You're the only reason I'm staying," she said. "Once you have your child I'll be finished."

This is exactly what I needed: a savior, someone to suffer with me, someone with whom I could share my burden.

"I have another lead," said Laura, segueing into the next topic of our conversation and at the same time relieving me of the anxiety connected with any consideration of Kerry's Guatemala gambit. "I've been doing a bit of footwork and have come up with a possibility at an out-of-state agency called The Children's Foundation."

The short of it was that Laura had also been scanning the photolistings of the ICCC and had come across three Colombian boys who had escaped my eye. "They're all eight years old," she added, but I hedged on this age group.

"I had really set six as the upper limit, Laura." I wanted a good running start before I had a teenager on my hands. "Anyway, how do we know they'll work with single men?"

"Because I called them," she said. "They'll work with single men on a case-by-case basis." She really had done her footwork.

"You'll have to travel to Colombia twice. The cost is seven thousand plus travel."

It sounded good and relatively inexpensive. "Give them a call," she said, sensing my interest. "The director is Tara Markey."

I called immediately and was greeted by a pleasant-sounding woman who sang my praises, having been primed by Laura. Then she launched into particulars. "Yes," she said. "We'll be happy to work with you."

"And the Colombians?"

"It's up to them," she said. "I just don't know what they'll say."

"Will you ask them?"

"Yes, as soon as I'm able to."

"When will that be?"

"When their telephone strike is over."

As far as I was concerned, once again Colombia was my only live iron in the fire. I was nowhere near recommitting myself to Kerry's care. Then I received a call from Mary at Adoption Unlimited, the woman who had attempted to help me with Costa Rica. I was flattered that she remembered me in such detail. "I've made a call on your behalf to Ilien Adoptions in Georgia," she said. "They have a Bolivian program for which you're eligible."

Bolivia. Hmmm. I had always wanted to visit Bolivia.

"They have three boys, all in the age group you're approved for: Johnny and José, both six, and Daniel, who's five."

"And they'll definitely allow a single man to adopt?"

"Definitely. These boys are ready to go."

"Mary," I said. "This is too good to be true. What's the program cost?"

"Fourteen thousand."

Silence.

It *was* too good to be true. I just could not make that kind of financial stretch. I had to draw the line somewhere and reminded myself that the figure did not even include airfare and miscellaneous fees. When I attended the information session at my agency fourteen months ago, I had estimated a personal outlay of around $5000, beyond which I would have to borrow. Three times that figure was simply not obtainable. I was already considering establishing a credit line on my house, but I did not know how much that would net me. Wistfully, but with a resolution born of having looked reality clear in the eyes, I bid *adiós* to Johnny, José, and Daniel.

Several days later I received a call from The Children's Foundation. Tara Markey had managed to reach Colombia, but she was not at all encouraging. "I get no feeling from them that a single man would work," she said. "It might not be worth the risk of time and money."

I was disappointed, of course, but I also appreciated that someone was looking out for me and my scarce finances. After a few words of affirmation and encouragement, we hung up and I closed the book on Colombia.

I now had no irons in the fire, although I still retained an option on Kerry's offer of Guatemala. I felt cornered. Incredulously, I began to warm to my own agency again, trying to concentrate on the idea of a child from the jungles of Guatemala rather than on the difficult personality who would act as facilitator. Then I remembered the package that had been passed to me regarding Guatemala's Children. I went to my now brimming adoption file and retrieved the paperwork. The cover letter was addressed to an official of the Department of Human Services of the State of Maine:

I want to thank you for your interest in adoption from Guatemala. Enclosed is information about Guatemala and this program.

First I will give you a bit of information on myself: I believe I was one of the first families to adopt privately in Southern California. At the time I began my search, most of the adoptions from Guatemala were through American-sponsored orphanages in Guatemala. They were closed down by the Guatemalan government in late 1987, and currently all of the adoptions from Guatemala are private adoptions.

I continued to help families after my return, and finally realized that in order to continue doing this (which I dearly love), I had to charge a fee for my services (90% of my fee goes to AT&T!). About a year after my return from Guatemala, I began to set up this program. In the past two years, 15 adoptions have been completed, and in the next few months 6 more babies will join their families. We are now awaiting the birth of 5 babies, some expected in the next couple of weeks, so at this time there is no wait for a referral. Although I refer to "babies" in my information, it is also possible to find toddlers and older children for families.

As far as adoption requirements for Guatemala—there are really very few. There are no age requirements, or marriage/divorce requirements, or religious, weight, or number of children in the family requirements. In fact, we are currently placing a baby with a single man.

In the information it states that it may take four to five months for an adoption to be completed, however the Guatemalan courts have recently been re-staffed with new judges and clerks, and it looks like the adoptions may be going more quickly and will be taking only three months now.

The letter was signed by a woman named Marilyn Kiley. The cost of the program approached the upper limit of what I felt I could afford. Everything sounded "right." Her letter bespoke experience and was optimistic. The Guatemalan process seemed uncomplicated. Best of all, Marilyn was a single adoptive parent herself. It was not long before I was on the phone with her.

Marilyn was enthusiastic, reflecting the tone of her letter. She was very talkative and had a raspy Carol Channing voice. Her expressions were Southern California ("man"). "It took a while," she said, "but my contact in Guatemala City, Jorge, has learned to accept the idea of single adoption."

I told her what I was looking for, the cadence of my speech set by her perfectly timed "Uh-huhs" on the other end of the line. "Everything I read in your package seems perfect," I said. "Is there any bad news?"

Marilyn laughed in her Carol Channing way. "There are no problems," she said. "But there is a potential delay. There are no waiting children, so Jorge would have to look for a child for you." She also added that the child might be a bit younger than I had anticipated. "Two to three years old," she said.

I reasoned that I could probably manage a three year old, but then I had to factor in daycare costs. However, I was at the point where I was willing to indulge in crisis management: I wanted the adoption now, I would deal with details later. I closed the conversation with a statement of serious interest and a promise to call the next day. Just before I hung up I heard a child screech in the background—Marilyn's adoptive daughter. I felt that I was dealing with a normal person living a normal family life.

So it was Guatemala now, either with Marilyn or (gasp) Kerry.

The next day Marilyn called *me*. She had phoned Jorge, her contact in Guatemala, just to double check the situation for me. He was willing to work with me. I immediately called Laura, telling her about my conversation with Marilyn, which I had had time to sleep on. "You sound like you've made up your mind," she said.

"I liked what I heard. Plus, and this is a big plus, Marilyn is a single adoptive parent, so I feel as if I've found a kindred spirit."

"What about Kerry?"

"What about her?"

Laura went on to explain that Kerry was waiting for my response to her Guatemala program.

"Laura," I said, "I don't think Kerry has a program. And I don't think she has any protocol in place for getting me a Guatemalan child. Thirdly, after the way I was handled with her Russian program, I don't have much faith in her ability to do anything for me anytime soon."

After a moment of silence Laura pressed closer to the phone. "You're very astute," she said, surreptitiously, as if Kerry might be somewhere in the vicinity. I was totally unmanned by this confidence. "Then should I tell her no?" she asked.

"Tell her no. But explain to her that it's because I've found a Guatemala program with a successful track record and a facilitator I've established a rapport with. I want to go with it."

Before hanging up I asked Laura to send my homestudy to Guatemala's Children.

Two days later I received a letter from Kerry stating that she wanted to FedEx my homestudy to Guatemala, even though, I learned later, Laura had already communicated my lack of interest to her. I immediately wrote back to inform her that I was going with another program, one that was willing to make inquiries on my behalf even before accepting me as a client.

Another two days passed, during which I was able to recoup some of my energy, dissipate some of my frustration, and take notice that things had sorted themselves out. I was dealing with one program that was both within my budget and willing to work with a single man. This was all I wanted.

One day shortly thereafter, while still waiting for word from Marilyn in California, I returned home to a message on my answering machine. It was from Kerry. "I have a child for you. Please call! Oh, it would be such a shame if you didn't call."

Where oh where was she getting these children from? The last time she tried this, it had angered me. Now I felt only annoyance at being handled like this: Every time I expressed frustration with her she was able to conjure up a child. I stared at the answering machine for a few moments, deliberating. Then I pressed "erase."

In her message Kerry had given me a choice. I opted for the shame.

—— Paddlin' with Marilyn ——

Kerry would not give up.

The next morning when I got to work there was another message on my machine: "Very important!"

Now I had to bite. I called Kerry and she practically leaped through the phone. "I want to describe this little Guatemalan boy to you!"

I listened. His name was Enrique: six years old (age forensically determined because there was no birth certificate), parents dead, brought to orphanage by eighty-year-old grandmother who could no longer care for him. He was in the first grade and appeared to be gifted in math. This is what most impressed me. As someone who has always struggled with math, I had the highest admiration for those to whom it came easy.

I asked Kerry what else she could tell me. Once I had posed the question I could feel her ease back a bit and become more businesslike, as if she sensed control returning to her hands.

"I have a fax right here," she said, "in which the caseworker describes Enrique as sweet and shy, physically and mentally sound."

"They have a fax machine in the jungle?"

"Uh-huh."

"What else?"

Now Kerry was in full command. "Well," she said, "he's in an orphanage in a remote part of Guatemala. I've been there myself. It's well run and the children are well cared for."

Damn it. I felt myself moving back onto the fence, hovering between Marilyn and Kerry. What is the old saying? Fool me once, shame on you, fool me twice, shame on me. I felt my dander rising, but only because I was angry for allowing myself to be wafted back toward Kerry's camp.

The line was silent for some time. Then I asked, "Where did you get this child, Kerry?"

"I've had him in the back of my file for about a year and finally got around to pulling him out."

Damn it again. She had this child all along and could have presented him to me earlier, much earlier, before all the disappointments and frustrations with other programs.

"So what do you think?" she asked.

I just could not allow myself to make any kind of snap decision, especially where Kerry was concerned. I was also in the throes of a swelling allegiance to Marilyn, with whom I had gotten off to a very good start. Then my thoughts returned to Enrique. "Could I see his picture?" I asked.

Silence.

"Why do you want a picture?" asked Kerry.

I was struck by this comment. Once again I felt that I was being told what was best for me. "Because," I said, "I want to look into Enrique's eyes and see if he speaks to me."

Kerry did not dwell for a moment on my reasoning. It was as if she could not connect with what I was saying. "I hate to think that your seeing his picture is going to make or break this adoption," she finally said.

"Then you think that I'm asking for too much?"

I could sense Kerry's ardor gaining strength. She wanted to argue the point. "It would take a month to get a picture up here."

"I thought you said they had a fax machine."

"Not a good one."

"Tell them to send it FedEx."

"That's not so easy."

The woman was protesting much too much. She did not even suspect that her manner was sending me back to Marilyn, her competitor. "Kerry," I said, cutting her off, "get me a picture. Good-bye."

That night I called Marilyn again. I told her about the sudden appearance of Enrique. "It sounds good," she said. "Are you going for it?"

I had harbored a degree of fear that Marilyn would resent my dealing with both her and my home agency in the Guatemalan arena at the same time. But her understanding words reassured me that her concern was that I was doing the right thing for me. "Marilyn," I said, "what do you think your role is in facilitating an adoption for me?"

Her reply was immediate. "I'm here to help you get the kind of child you're looking for."

That was it. Exactly. "When you find a child for me, will I receive a picture as well?"

Marilyn laughed her raspy Carol Channing laugh, as if she were about to break into a chorus of "Hello, Dolly!" "You'll probably get a video," she said.

That did it. Marilyn saw herself as working for me. Kerry treated me more like a subject who should be grateful for small favors. Instead of a handful of adoption "possibilities" from Albania to Peru, I was now on the verge of committing myself to one very promising program. It was clear that I had made up my mind to go with Marilyn. The only thing lacking was the formal yes.

That night I slept well for the first time in weeks. Fourteen months had passed since my initial orientation, and at last things seemed to be coming together for me. I was a single man who would be advocated for by a single adoptive parent. I would call Kerry the next day and tell her I was not going to pursue an adoption through her. I just could not bear to be handled by her any longer. I knew that Enrique, if he was as good as Kerry had made him out to be, would find a loving home.

Incredulously, the next day I received a thick envelope from Kerry. She was continuing her frontal assault. The envelope contained a report from Casa de Guatemala, Enrique's orphanage. It was a barely legible fax, in Spanish. Kerry had affixed a Post-It note: "The orphanage director will take new photos of child this weekend."

I read the fax in detail. Kerry had told me the boy was six. The form said seven. How old would he be by the time I got him?

There was another memo posted to the paperwork: "I'll be at a meeting in Bangor today, so don't call until tomorrow."

Kerry was coming on like a freight train. Why did she think I would call at all? The package told me nothing that she herself had not communicated.

I called Laura to tell her my troubles. "Laura," I said, "I need someone to know that I am not leaning toward adopting Enrique. In fact, I've already made up my mind to go with Marilyn in California."

"Have you told Kerry and Marilyn of your decision yet?"

"No. It's this picture thing with Kerry."

"I heard."

"Laura, do you think I'm wrong in asking for a picture?"

"You're not wrong at all. Many families adopt without seeing a picture first, but they're usually looking for infants. Most families feel the way you do."

I needed to make myself clear on this point. It was not so much the picture as Kerry's attitude toward my request. "She made me feel that if I didn't adopt this little boy, I would be responsible for his ongoing misery and abandonment."

"I don't think he's miserable."

"Neither do I. But, my God, every child is not the perfect kid for me. Yet that's how Kerry is trying to make me feel. She seems to be able to come up with kids at will, and she expects me to snap them up on her say-so."

We both paused in silence to take a breath, and then, "Bob, I don't want you to feel cornered."

"I refuse to feel cornered."

That night Marilyn called me. "How's it going?" she asked.

I told her about Enrique and that I was waiting for his picture, but that I was not leaning toward him because of his age. "I'll get back to you as soon as possible."

The next day I received yet more mail from Kerry, a contract stating my agreement to adopt Enrique and to look after all of his material needs and to provide him with attention and love. At the bottom was a space for my signature. If I signed this paper I would be committed. In spite of all my protestations and leeriness, Kerry had blindly gone ahead and processed the paperwork for this adoption. I was now convinced that she was not acting in my best interest. She simply did not want one of her clients to defect to another program. Yet, ironically, she had worked diligently to discourage me from placing any trust in her. The bottom line was that Marilyn allowed me to feel that I had some say and control over events. With Kerry I was an unwitting passenger, like a remora clamped to a shark's belly.

I sat down and wrote a letter to Kerry declining, with regret, her referral of Enrique.

Now my thoughts were free to concentrate on Marilyn and her program. Once I had taken the step of declining Kerry's help, I felt suddenly unencumbered and able to think again. However, now that I was able to consider Marilyn's program on its own merits and not merely as an alternative to Kerry, important questions about Guatemala's Children began to surface. I was most concerned about where Marilyn's children came from. She did not work with orphanages; she had made this clear in the cover letter of her package. Where, then, did she get these kids?

I called her. "Marilyn, I've written a letter to my home agency, declining their referral. But I haven't mailed it yet. I need to ask you a couple of questions before I say yes to your program."

"Shoot."

I mentioned my concern about the source of the children. Marilyn told me that Jorge, her Guatemalan contact, had a tried-and-true network of families. "He puts the word out and usually comes up with a child in three to four months."

"Are these kids given up by their families for money?" I was haunted by a vision of some little boy being pulled, kicking and screaming, from the arms of his poverty-stricken mother.

Marilyn connected with my concern. "It's not what you think," she said. "There are cases of destitution or near-abandonment."

I was suddenly panic stricken. If a child was destitute, why could I not simply send the family $200 a month to care for his needs? This would enable him to remain with a family he already knew and loved.

"Marilyn," I said, "I've been involved in the adoption process long enough now to know what I'm doing. But I haven't stared a private adoption in the face yet. I need time to think about it."

Marilyn, of course, was willing to give me all the time I needed. Once again I was passing sleepless nights. I did not want to be the cause of the removal of a child from his family, no matter how willing they were to give him up.

It occurred to me that I knew a couple who had recently completed a private adoption in Haiti. They were the same people who had passed on Marilyn's information package to me. The next day I called Martha, who, with her husband Don, had written one of my reference letters. She was a big booster of my efforts. Both were very savvy veterans of the adoption process, having three adoptive children of various races of their own.

Martha was happy to speak with me, and almost everything she said was something to take home. She described the adoption of her son, Daniel, from Haiti. Daniel had been brought to an orphanage by an aged relative who was not able to care for him.

I raised the theoretical $200-a-month issue. Martha bit immediately. "In Haiti that money wouldn't have made a difference," she said. "Because it wouldn't have bought him the opportunities he has here for a healthy and happy life. That's why this relative gave him up, so Daniel would have an opportunity for a better life."

I took comfort in this. I pictured a little Guatemalan boy, ill fed, poorly clothed, and with little hope of a decent education, living with people for whom even life without a child was an ongoing misfortune. My mind needed to conjure up such images if I was to go on. Martha sensed some residual unease, however. She made a valuable suggestion. "Look, ask Marilyn to place a priority on a kid in an orphanage or who is living with aged grandparents or relatives unable to care for him. See what your options are and the limits of what she can do for you."

This was advice I could use. I called Laura and told her where I was at emotionally. "Private adoptions go on all the time," she said, "and I've never personally known one that turned out to be anything like what you fear."

I mentioned my conversation with Martha and how it had substantially diminished my fear. Then Laura told me something that gave me the confidence I needed to gird my loins and proceed with Marilyn's program. Laura had called the ICCC on my behalf. "I asked about Marilyn Kiley," she said, "and they've had no complaints about her. She's been very successful in placing children."

That was it, then. I called Marilyn the next day and asked if she would be willing to first look for a child in an orphanage and, failing that, ask her contact to seek out a child who is in a near-abandonment situation. She reminded me that she did not work with orphanages because she believed adoption in Guatemala to be impossible via that route. "But I'll tell Jorge," she said. "And don't worry, everything will be okay."

"I know it will," I said. "I think this is my last chance at success."

Marilyn told me that she had received my homestudy and some pictures of me and my home from Laura. "I'll send you some paperwork tomorrow," she said. "Don't worry."

I stopped worrying. I really did.

That evening I took a walk and mailed my letter to Kerry. But on the way home all I could think about was Enrique. I found solace in the assumption that he had no idea that someone like me even walked the earth.

Guatemala's Children

June 1992: I moved into my fifteenth month of the adoption process hoping I would never have another month like the fourteenth. I felt as if I had sailed out of a storm and was now standing on deck on a bluebird day, looking back on a violent miscegenation of swirling clouds and angry seas that I was lucky to have survived.

Kerry finally gave up on me. At least there were no more phone calls or letters. But through Laura she made the magnanimous offer to work with me on a Guatemalan adoption should my experience with Marilyn not prove fruitful. I was surprised at how far such a gesture went toward redeeming her in my eyes.

In the interim Marilyn had sent me a list of documents I needed to complete for her program:

Medical report
Employer letter
Birth certificate, certified copies (two)
Copy of *notarized* homestudy
Statement from local police that I had no criminal record

All right, I thought, now I have something *in my hands,* something doable. Now, for a while at least, I would be controlling the pace of the process. Because I was born in New Jersey, I had to send to Trenton for the certified birth certificates. That's right, work logically, I thought. First address the things that will take the longest. While I was shuffling Marilyn's papers, I received a response from the INS on my I-600A:

IT HAS BEEN DETERMINED THAT YOU ARE ABLE TO FURNISH PROPER CARE TO AN ORPHAN OR ORPHANS AS DEFINED BY SECTION 101(b) (1) (F) OF THE IMMIGRATION AND NATIONALITY ACT.

I had been approved. This meant that, officially, the way was paved for bringing my future son into the United States. This approval was good for one year. Before that time expired I would have to identify the specific child I had in mind and then file an I-600, "Petition to Classify Orphan as an Immediate Relative."

To me this was a sign, of sorts, that the government expected me to adopt within a year. In my mind an outer limit had been established—a time frame that seemed to presume a successful outcome. Because Marilyn had indicated the referral of a child in three to four months, I had time to spare. Was a year a long time? I could not decide whether it was too long to wait. All I knew was that by tomorrow morning it would be less than a year and the clock would continue to run from there, bringing me ever closer to my son.

After having sent my request for copies of my birth certificate to Trenton, I went off to the local police station—a place I had never been before—to ask them for a letter stating that I had no criminal record. I lived in a small town. Small-town police departments are wonderful, because any request, no matter how trivial, is handled with gravity and decorum, as a sort of practice for the murder or street riot they hoped would occur during their professional lives.

When I walked into the small brick building, the chief of police himself was sitting behind his desk, polishing a pistol that I am sure had never been fired in the line of duty. Tacked to the bulletin board were wanted posters of desperate-looking people from other states, people who probably had little inkling where Maine was and, therefore, with whom the chief would never have to deal. But guns and wanted posters are part of the reason people become police officers. However, in this small town the police blotter of the daily paper carries items such as "The police emergency rescue team responded to a report of a body in the river. But when they got there it was discovered to be a log." Or "Mrs. Elsie Beal reported seeing a hand outside her kitchen window. Police responded but were unable to find anything amiss."

In this light, the chief was happy to see me. When I told him why I needed the letter he was so kind and complimentary. "You'll have to bring him by when you get him. I'll show him around. Maybe he'd like to see a police car."

I was sure he would like to see a police car, and I was sure the chief would have the time to show it to him. I stood quietly by while the chief took down my name and address. After running the check he returned, took out a letterhead, and typed up his statement: "The above subject has no criminal record on file at the Orono Police Department."

I watched as he signed it and then lovingly blew on the signature. Then he handed it to me. "There you go," he said.

There I go. Beautiful words. I was moved by his care and patience. "What do I owe you?" I asked.

The chief waved me off. "No charge."

No charge. Even more beautiful words. He was the first person I had met on the adoption thoroughfare who did not have his hand out.

I went home and slipped the police letter into a manila folder labeled "Marilyn." Then I called for an appointment for a physical because the physical I had submitted with my initial application was now outdated. I was able to get one that very day. Small-town clinics are as wonderful as small-town police stations: unhurried, purposeful, safe.

The secretaries at the clinic were elated to hear of my plans. The three women threw adoring looks at me, as if by adopting I was the one who was finally going to put the world in order.

My physician was the chatty type; he was young, bright, and independent minded. I always felt that I was the very patient he had been waiting for to bounce ideas off of or to challenge with his own unorthodox thoughts about healing or the influence of the Thai language on American English. Because I was also young, bright, and independent minded, I had a lot of ideas of my own and on the very same topics (except the Thai). We usually wound up talking *at* each other, sort of like a shoot-out, until one or the other of us ran out of breath. Dr. Riley took the news of my adoption in stride. "But you're single, aren't you?" he asked.

"Yes."

"Well," he said, still looking over my chart, "isn't that difficult?

"What," I chided, "being single?"

The doctor looked at me. "No, adopting as a single."

I shrugged. "There have been ups and downs."

I asked the good doctor if he would like to be my son's physician. I made sure he knew that this would be a Hispanic child, probably with dark skin. I was looking for the slightest sign of discomfort in his speech or manner. There had been stories of physicians who did not interact well with children of other "races," and I wanted to know up front whether this would be a problem. As expected, Dr. Riley saw the adoption simply as the acquisition of another patient. "I'd be honored to be your son's physician," he said.

After the physical I asked to have my shots updated, which was recommended for Guatemala. I received a tetanus booster and a hepatitis-B vaccination. Before leaving, the secretary notarized the physical examination report. As I exited the clinic with my receipt in hand, I noticed that I had not been charged for the shots—another gesture of support, another small kindness from people who cared about what I was doing. I needed this, especially now when I was drawing closer to my son with every form I mailed, every check I wrote.

The reference letter from my employer was the slow step in the application process. The chairperson of my department at the university was away for most of the summer. I really did need his signature on a document stating my place of employment, capacity, performance, and salary. I also had to wait to receive the birth certificate copies from Trenton. The delay in obtaining these two items meant that my July was quiescent, with absolutely no activity on the adoption front. Interestingly enough, though, during this time I received a call from Dave Penn, the banker who had an interest in Guatemalan adoptions. He just wanted to know how things were going. I was flattered by his continued interest, pleased to have someone to think aloud to as well.

Dave listened as I described my involvement with Guatemala's Children. He thought it strange that Marilyn did not deal with orphanages. "We adopted our last boy from a Guatemalan orphanage in 1990," he said.

This *was* strange. Marilyn had made it clear to me that all adoptions from Guatemala were now private. If, indeed, it was possible to adopt from an orphanage, why was she not aware of it? These thoughts rekindled troubling images of children being separated from their parents. I expressed this concern to Dave; he felt that I had nothing to fear. "There are abundant abandonment and incipient abandonment situations in Guatemala," he assured me. "Your scenario of a child being torn from his mother's arms is an unlikely one."

I needed to have this reinforced; and I needed to hear it from people in the know. Was I being overcautious in questioning the propriety of a private adoption in Guatemala? Perhaps my concerns were unfounded.

By the middle of August 1992—seventeen months into the adoption process—I had all my documents for Marilyn in hand. All the signatures had been notarized and I took a special pleasure in running my fingers over the raised seals. Little did these notaries suspect that by their solemn acts of office they were helping me to create my own little family.

I sent the package of documents to Marilyn along with her first payment of $500—another wee little bird. That evening I called to tell her that the material was on the way. When I told her I had enclosed a $500 money order, she sighed. "There's been an increase," she said.

Her comment did not register with me right off. "Increase?"

"Yeah. Jorge has been complaining of escalating costs in Guatemala, so he's insisting on more money."

I swallowed hard, girding myself for the bad news. "How much more?"

"Fifteen hundred."

I fell silent, thinking hard for several moments. Should I be suspicious about this? Was I face to face with an adoption scandal? No, Laura had called ICCC and Marilyn was clean. A lot of couples had successfully adopted through her.

"Marilyn," I said. "This really takes me by surprise. I can't just take a thousand-dollar increase in stride. This is a lot of money for me."

Marilyn commiserated, but it was not the type of commiseration from which I drew strength. "I know, I know," she said, "it would be a lot of money for me, too." Marilyn suddenly sounded weary. In the background her daughter was ranting. Every few seconds Marilyn would excuse herself to scream at the child.

"Ouch!" she suddenly exclaimed.

"Are you okay?" I asked.

"Yes," she said. "I mean no. I just burned myself. I poured hot water on my hand. I was making coffee. Geez."

I soon found myself at the receiving end of a manic monologue about the perils of living in Los Angeles, even though this had nothing to do with either adoption or scalding water. I made an attempt to get Marilyn back on track.

"I need a promise that this increase will be the last. If Jorge decides to increase his fee again, I want to be grandfathered in at the current fee."

"I understand," said Marilyn before pausing to scream at her daughter again.

I realized immediately that I had received understanding and not a promise. Yet I did not press Marilyn. She was the horse I had all my money on. She was the only horse in the race. I asked once again about the possibility of an orphanage adoption.

"I spoke to Jorge," she said, in a manner suggesting that if I had not raised the point she would not have either. "He says an orphanage adoption isn't possible, but that in cases where it is possible it can take up to one and a half years."

My head was spinning. An orphanage adoption was not possible except in cases where it was possible? One and a half years? Was I being "handled" in some way? Had she really talked to Jorge? My doubts were not strong at this point, because I wanted to believe only the best about the people and the program. But Marilyn suddenly seemed like a somewhat different person. The original-recipe Marilyn had been focused and knowledgeable. This extra-crispy version was scattered and uncertain of her facts. Then another tear in the firmament: "Did you send me photocopies of those documents?" she asked.

"What do you mean? Photocopies along with the originals?"

"No, just photocopies."

"I sent you only the originals. I kept photocopies of everything."

"I'll have to send the originals back to you."

"Why?"

"Because you have to have them apostilled by your secretary of state."

"Apostilled?"

"Yeah. The secretary of state has to verify that your notaries are really notaries."

"With names like Hattie Osnoe and Maude Tweetie?" I said. "What else could they be?"

"You need to do it."

I leaned into the phone. "Why didn't you tell me this, Marilyn?"

Another juvenile screech from the other end of the line. "Annie, shut up!" rasped Marilyn. I could picture her rubbing her scalded hand against her forehead, as if to say, "God give me the strength! Kids!"

Before I knew it Marilyn had involved me in a conversation about her life as a legal secretary, which was her "real" job, but one that had her at her wits' end and that she was on the brink of abandoning in favor of full-time adoption work. At this point I was ready to yell "Uncle." I felt a rising need to get off the line. The easiest thing to do was to simply await the return of my documents and then dutifully have them apostilled.

"One more thing," she said, as I sighed and listened. "I'm sending you two more documents."

"That's *two* more things," I said.

"A power of attorney authorizing Jorge to proceed with the adoption paperwork on your behalf and declarations that you'll have to give to the people who wrote your letters of reference."

"Declarations?"

"Yeah. All three declarations are the same. They just state that they know you and that you would make a good parent."

"Then what were the letters of reference all about?"

"Hey, this is Guatemala," she said, as if I should have known better.

I made it a point to ask whether they would have to be both notarized and apostilled. "Have we forgotten anything else?" I asked.

"That's it for now." And then, "ANNIEEEEEEE!"

By September I really did have all my documents in hand—each one of them notarized. In the meantime, Marilyn had sent me even more forms, including a name form (verifying that I am who I am) and an affidavit of financial support (verifying that I can afford to take care of a child). All told, I now had a portfolio of ten documents. Marilyn assured me that I finally had all of them.

I drove down to Augusta, eighty miles away, and found the office of the secretary of state with little problem. Apostilles of the ten notarizations cost $10 per page. "It will take about an hour," the woman behind the counter said.

I used the interim to avail myself of the Maine State Library, just across the street from the state house. As I scanned the shelves in the periodicals room, I came across an article about a single man who had adopted a nine-year-old boy from Paraguay. It contained a formal portrait of the proud father and son, both beaming into the camera lens. I averted my eyes for a moment and thought of myself with my own arm slung around a little brown-skinned boy's shoulder and his lean arm around my waist. I blessed this man and his sweet success in Paraguay. I could see in both his and his son's eyes that in some magical way the right man and the right boy had been brought together. That is something Laura had told me early on: "The right parents and the right children tend to find one another."

When I returned to the secretary of state's office they were just finishing up with my documents. The clerk who brought them out set them in front of me. Each bore an immense cobalt blue seal—very impressive, certainly worth ten bucks.

"I was able to do nine of them," he said.

"Nine? But I gave you ten documents."

"Yes," he said. "But this one here. . . ." I watched as he fished out the homestudy. "This one here couldn't be apostilled."

"But it's notarized," I said, taking it from his hands and pointing to the last page.

"Yes," he said, patiently. "But the signature is a photocopy. It has to be an original for us to apostille it."

I waited until I had left the office before giving vent to my ire. I was angry. The homestudy! Of all things! It was as if Marilyn and my agency were in cahoots. They were perfect for one another. Perhaps they should form an adoptive relationship.

I immediately sought out a phone booth and called Laura, telling her what had happened.

"What an oversight," she said. I could feel the sympathy in her voice, but it was not enough this time.

"It's not an oversight, Laura," I said. "This is just sloppy work. An oversight is using a colon when a semicolon is called for. But sending me a homestudy with an original signature should be a given. I mean, I sense that the agency knew I had been sent this copy and that it was okay."

What could she say? "We'll send another last page with an original signature right away."

I was still angry, because I would have to make another day of it in Augusta. I did not know how soon I would be able to do that. But I also did not want to be one of those people who rant and rave when nothing at the moment could be done. So I ended the call by expressing the hope that Laura and I would meet sometime soon (we had never had a face-to-face conversation), and Laura expressed the same sentiment.

I made the long drive home still feeling frustrated, as if I were shouldering my share of the adoption work just fine but the experts were having a hard time getting things right.

We were deep into September now. The days were still powerfully warm but cooled down dramatically as evening came on, auguring the winter to come. When I arrived home I walked over to the river bank and looked out over the mirror finish of the still water and then over to the silver maples turning gold. Then I took some consolation in the fact that I had gotten ninety percent of my documents apostilled that day. Standing down by the river allowed me to look at what I had rather than what I had come away without. Next week, no doubt, I would be able to go to Augusta again.

When I entered the house there was a message on my answering machine—from Marilyn. She had lost the $500 money order I had sent her. "Could you send another?"

Nearer My Son to Thee

The last page of my homestudy with an *original* signature arrived as I moved into my nineteenth month of the adoption process. It was another few days before I could see my way clear to travel to Augusta. In the interim Marilyn called to check in on me.

"Thanks for the second money order," she said. "I don't know where I put the first one."

"So you did receive it?"

"Oh yes," she said. "But I just don't know what I did with it."

"It doesn't matter," I said. "I've stopped payment on it, so it's moot."

I had, indeed, gone to the bank to verify that the original money order had not been cashed, and I had stopped payment on it. What is the saying President Reagan used to attribute to the Russians? Trust but verify? In any case, my mentioning the stop payment was a subtle way, I hoped, of reminding Marilyn that this is business and I intended to keep track of my money.

“What’s next?” I asked.

“Do you have all your documents apostilled by your secretary of state?”

“Except for the homestudy. I’ll have that finished in a couple of days.”

“Good,” she said, in what seemed to be a return to lucidity. “You’ll need to send all ten documents to the Guatemalan consulate in New York to have the apostilles authenticated.”

This was beginning to sound like a scene from the Marx Brothers classic, “A Day at the Races,” where Chico peddles a winning horse’s encrypted name to Groucho, but the name is useless without the code book, and the code book is useless without the breeders guide, and so on.

“So,” I said, “the notarizations have to be apostilled and the apostilles have to be authenticated.”

“Right,” said Marilyn, instructively, like a schoolmarm who has finally gotten through to a dunderheaded student. “And don’t forget to ask about a visa. You’ll need to send your passport to the consulate. You can get a visa good for either one year or five years.”

I asked Marilyn what the difference in cost was.

“It’s free,” she said.

“You’re kidding.”

“No.”

“Well, then, I’ll take the five years.”

I called the Guatemalan consulate that very day. The man who answered was very polite and understood immediately what I needed. I had feared I would have to tell him my frustrating story from the beginning.

The cost for the authentications of the apostilled notarizations was $10 per page. It was as if the U.S. and Guatemalan governments were collaborating, one whispering to the other, “Ten bucks! Tell him ten bucks!” Perhaps the free visa was a ploy to mollify me, to give me a little something for nothing so I would be less resistant about sending $100 with my dossier.

A couple of days later I was en route to Augusta again, with one flimsy homestudy page in hand. I walked up to the counter in the office of the secretary of state and waited my turn. Standing next to me was a woman in her late thirties, very pleasant looking, who seemed to be craning her neck ever so subtly to see what I was serving up. I shifted my eyes toward her and turned my head a tad as well, but not enough to allow her to suspect that I suspected that she was trying to see what my paperwork was all about. Then she spoke. “Ah, I see you’re using the same agency I am.”

“Are you adopting too?” I asked.

"This is my second son," she said. "The first was from Ecuador, this one's coming from Paraguay." Her eyes begged for reciprocal information, which I had no problem with because I immediately considered her another member of "the club"—and a veteran, no less.

"Mine is coming from Guatemala," I said, as if speaking with certainty would make it a matter of fact.

"Oh, I've heard about Kerry's Guatemala program," she said. "But I didn't think it was active yet."

"Kerry has no Guatemala program," I said, without rancor. "I'm working with an independent facilitator."

"How's it going?"

"So far so good. Being a single makes it a little difficult at times, though." I tried to state this without begging admittance to the cult of victimhood.

"Not if you're a woman," she said. "Then it's easy."

So, she was single, a kindred spirit. I asked her what she did for a living.

"I teach grammar school in a small town."

"How is your son doing?"

The woman laughed. "Just fine. And I'm doing better, too."

"Better?" I asked, my eyes soliciting clarification.

"In small Maine towns it's not okay to be a single woman but it is okay to be a single mother."

The clerk came up to me and I handed her my homestudy. "Do you have a lot of documents?" asked the woman adopting from Paraguay.

I told her that, relatively speaking, ten was not many.

"Do you need a psych eval?"

"I don't think so. Do you?"

"When I adopted from Ecuador I was interviewed by a psychologist there, and then, out of the blue, they made me take a written diagnostic test as well. I guess they'll do the same thing this time, too."

It suddenly struck me as strange that I had not been asked to undergo some sort of clinical evaluation, especially as a single man. But I was certainly not going to raise the issue.

Before our conversation ended, the clerk had returned with my apostilled homestudy page—another cobalt blue starburst, very eye-catching, very official looking. Martha, my friend who together with her husband Don had adopted from Haiti, had told me that the more spangles the better when dealing with Third World countries. "Ribbons, seals, stamps, colored ink," she had advised. "They like that stuff."

The next day I went to FedEx and sent my dossier off to the Guatemalan consulate along with a money order for $100. When I handed the envelope over, I felt a palpable weight of preoccupation lift from my mind. The hard work was now over. All the documentation had been obtained. The Guatemalans would now rubber stamp it.

At about this time I received a letter from Marilyn, who was infinitely easier to deal with on paper because her presentation in print was saner:

> When all of your documents have been returned to you, make a photocopy of everything. Copy the documents, and turn back any attachments, then photocopy the attachments, both sides, if there is a stamp or signature on the back side of the attachments. These photocopies are for your files. At this point you will need to send Jorge the first part of his fee—$3000. Three certified checks or bank money orders, whichever your bank does, will be fine.
>
> Then call me and we will figure out where to send everything to Jorge—either to Guatemala or here—since I think that about that time he may be here. I'm getting really excited that your package is almost complete, and you will be beginning the next process, which means that you will be a dad (and mom) in the not-too-distant future.

And then a dreadful thought struck me: what if the consulate loses my dossier? Oh, my God. The woman I had met at the state house who was adopting from Paraguay told me this had happened to her once and she had to have everything done over. I had made photocopies of everything I had sent, of course, but these were for my files and had no official capacity to expedite anything.

My fear was unjustified. As the twentieth month of my gestation dawned I watched as a red, white, and blue FedEx truck pulled up in front of my house. A minute later I had my dossier in hand: notarized, apostilled, and authenticated. I called Marilyn that evening and she told me to send everything to Guatemala. She added that I owed her the second half of her fee as well—$500.

The next day I completed my monetary transactions: $3000 for Jorge and $500 for Marilyn. Most of my liquid resources were now gone, and there was still more than $4000 to be paid out. Before traveling to Guatemala I would be able to bank a little more money, but I needed a cushion. At this point I was reminded of a quote attributed to the eccentric American fantasy writer, H. P. Lovecraft: "I wish I knew how people managed to get cash!"

I went down to my bank and inquired about a home equity line of credit. Based on the value of my home, I qualified for an upper limit of $5000. Gee, that was it? I took some comfort in realizing that I had a gamut of credit cards at my disposal, if one could call that comfort. With times being what they were, I took the $5000 credit line and received a checkbook to go with the account. Once again, collecting returnable bottles and cans welled with appeal for me. On a good day I could clear $15.

Now the long wait began. I had done everything expected of me, and an odd, unsettling mental state set in. I was no longer occupied by adoption-related paperwork, and with nothing concrete to do in that arena, the days, though unusually long, were pregnant with a subtle tension. At some point I would receive a call from Jorge or Marilyn and be expected to drop everything and head for Guatemala on the spur of the moment. I was going to have a child. It was going to happen soon.

On November 30, exactly four weeks after sending my dossier to Jorge, I received a call at work from Marilyn. "Jorge tried to reach you," she said flatly, almost like a rebuke.

"Where?" I pleaded.

"At your home. He has a two-year-old Ladino child he wants to offer you."(Ladino means the child has more European than Indian blood.)

My heart soared and then it sank. "Two is a little young, Marilyn," I said. "Besides, I'm not approved for a two year old." But I was not shattered by this loss, because I finally had a real, honest-to-goodness sign that Jorge was, indeed, trying to find a child for me. He was not a crook. I do not think I had ever abolished the possibility, until then.

Marilyn continued. "I think he's having trouble finding an older child."

"It hasn't been very long," I said. "For some reason I have faith in his efforts."

In the background, Marilyn's daughter screamed. Marilyn screamed back. "She's making popcorn!" she lamented. "Popcorn! It's all over the place!"

Marilyn Jekyll had vanished and once again I had Marilyn Hyde on the phone. "I've got to get out of this neighborhood!"

"Do you think you'll find one without popcorn?" I joked.

Marilyn didn't get it. "What do you mean?" she asked.

Marilyn was not a humorless woman. The difficulty was that she was the only one capable of making herself laugh.

"Is Jorge going to call me?" I asked.

"I hope so."

"What did he say?"

Even over the phone I could feel Marilyn shrug. "He didn't say anything, only that he had this child. . . . ANNIEEE! Oh, my God!"

"What!" I said, pressing my mouth to the receiver. "What's she doing?" I felt some small need to empathize with Marilyn's concerns, though my enthusiasm was not of the blood.

"Anyway," said Marilyn, suddenly composed, "just sit tight. It usually takes three to four months."

"That was my understanding," I said, willing to wait that long, if only because it would forestall my having to dispense home equity funds. I was also thinking of all the cans and bottles I could collect.

I had entered my twenty-first month of the adoption process. I was wondering how Billy and the others from the parenting classes were making out. I wondered hard about this at times, but never to the extent that I wanted to pick up the phone. At this point, I did not want to hear anything that would make it more difficult for me.

Who Took the Lid off Hell?

For three months all remained quiet on the adoption front. At first I was grateful for the respite. I once again relapsed into a state of mind where adoption dwelled on the periphery of conscious thought. I became quietly expectant, and I was able to conduct my life without jumping every time the phone rang.

But March 1993 was the second anniversary of my involvement in the process. Two years. This weighed heavily on my mind. I found myself once again willing the phone to ring, in the hope, of course, that it would be either Marilyn or Jorge. Finally, I could not stand it anymore and late in the month I picked up the phone myself. When I greeted Marilyn she sighed. Then she dropped the bomb: Jorge had been unreachable for several weeks.

"What!"

That was me, not wasting time in measuring my response, but giving immediate vent to my rage.

"I don't know what's going on," said Marilyn lackadaisically. "He's usually reliable. Sometimes."

"Usually reliable sometimes?" I echoed. "What does that mean? Marilyn! I sent him three thousand dollars!"

"I've tried calling him, but nobody picks up the phone," she explained.

"You seem to be suggesting that there is somebody there to pick up the phone. Do you think he's ignoring you?"

"I don't know," she said, absently.

"Well, let's try again," I said. "Let's call him, right now."

Marilyn hummed. "I don't speak Spanish," she said.

"I thought Jorge spoke English."

"Oh, he does, but his wife and daughter don't, and they might be the only ones home. Now, if we had someone who spoke Spanish, like my friend Dolores. . . ."

"Marilyn!" I cried. "Remember me? I speak Spanish!"

"Oh!" she exclaimed, as if it was all coming back to her. "Then let's call."

We quickly arranged a three-party call. After punching in a long string of numbers the phone began to ring—a foreign, grating rattle. I collected my thoughts and tried to calm myself. By the time the phone had rung six times my anticipation of an answer began to diminish. After the tenth ring Marilyn said, "Uh-uh." We abandoned the effort, for the moment.

"Marilyn," I said, "I'm very upset."

"Well, I am too," she concurred. Only the difference between our upsetedness was that she was $1000 better for it and I was $4000 poorer. Hell, if I thought I had four grand worth of leeway I would have adopted the Bolivian boys!

Finally, Marilyn made a more realistic attempt to assuage my nerves. "He has family in the States," she said. "He could very well be here visiting. And he's dealing with several other clients I've sent him."

"Do they know he's been incommunicado?"

"Hmmm?"

"Unreachable."

"Oh, no," she pleaded.

"Shouldn't you tell them?"

"Not yet," she said. "I want to give him more time."

I realized that Marilyn would not have told me about Jorge either had I not called her. Apparently these other clients had a more abiding faith in her than I and were willing to wait indefinitely before making inquiries. I felt as if someone had taken the lid off hell and I was teetering on the brink of the inferno. "Marilyn," I said, "what are you going to do now?"

"Keep trying," she said. "What else can I do? If I had the money I'd fly down and knock on his door. But I don't have any money."

"What about the thousand dollars I sent you?"

"Gone. For expenses."

After my conversation with Marilyn I immediately called Laura, feeling as if I were running home to mother with a hurt. I was embarrassed to call, because I felt that she would see me as a sucker for dealing with an independent facilitator three thousand miles away. More than that, I could already hear Kerry chanting, "So there!" Now I might have to crawl back to her and grovel for her help with another program.

As it turned out, Laura was very matter-of-fact about the whole thing. She seemed ready to forget about Marilyn and move on to other possibilities. I was strangely grateful for this attitude, because it meant she was not going to dwell on what she obviously considered to be a lost cause. It seemed she had seen this happen many times before and was no longer surprised by anything. But then there was the matter of my money. My money!

"I don't think you should expect to see that again," she said.

"But I *do* expect to see it again, Laura," I explained. "I mean, this guy Jorge has been successfully completing adoptions for years. Why should he pick me to swindle, especially when he could have gotten even more money out of me? My God, he could have gotten the rest of the money when I went to Guatemala and then stranded me there."

"That's right," she concurred. I did not know whether she was agreeing with me or simply affirming my reactions. "You know, there's a new organization in Portland that's starting a Polish program. . . ."

I hung my head in despair and squatted on the kitchen floor, taking the receiver with me. I just would not hear of Poland again. I was not up to it. I wanted Jorge to be back on the job and I wanted to know that he was still working for me. Or maybe I wished I could just get my money back and be done with him. Or maybe I didn't know what I wanted anymore.

Nine days later, I called Marilyn, unable to wait another minute. She had still been unable to contact Jorge, although, from the manner in which she said this I sensed that she had not tried. "This doesn't sound good at all," I despaired.

"I know," she said, offhandedly, and I pictured her doing her nails as she spoke with me.

I exploded. "Marilyn, I want my money back and I expect you to help me. I gave you a thousand dollars for nothing. Nothing! For a thousand dollars you put me in touch with a crook and a jackass. If I don't hear something soon I'm going to write every organization in the country that has anything to do with adoption and tell them my story!"

Marilyn took a modicum of umbrage. "Well," she said, "I hope you won't mention my name."

"Marilyn!" I cried. "Of course I'm going to mention your name! That's the point!"

It suddenly dawned on me—I was dealing with a kook.

In the interim I had received another source list from the Committee for Single Adoptive Parents. The thought of starting from scratch yet again, after two years of work, was breaking my heart. Poland, Costa Rica, Colombia, Russia, Guatemala. . . . I had failed with all of them, or perhaps some had failed me. Where would I turn now? Albania? Why not? I was willing to try anything. Perhaps I needed to consider a much younger or a much older child. But when I envisioned a fourteen year old materializing in my living room my spirits sank again.

Against the counsel of my instincts I plopped down on the sofa and opened the source list. I had learned how to read it in an abridged fashion, skipping to the line under each agency that indicated eligibility. *No men. No men. No men.* Perhaps I had the wrong source list, the one from the Committee for Single Adoptive Women? And then, *men accepted.*

I looked at the agency: Rainbow House, New Mexico, a Russian program. Oh, no. Not Russia again. What was the hitch? Perhaps they accepted only men who really wanted to be women. It must be the cost, I thought. That must be it. But no, $9000. I could not believe this agency could find a child for me when I knew that, even as I sat at home reading my source list, American couples were flooding into Russia and raiding the orphanages. I had even read about Americans who went to that country with no agency representation, no connections, no paperwork, and showed up at orphanages to "take their pick." Perhaps, then, the Russian children who were available to single men were those with serious birth defects or other disabilities. Could I deal with this?

I called Laura. "What do you know about Rainbow House?" I asked.

"Very good agency," she said. "We've worked with them before. They have a wonderful track record."

I told her about the information I had garnered from the CSAP source list. "There's got to be a hitch," I said. "When I was dealing with Kerry's Russian program she had mentioned that the Russians prioritize traditional families over singles and that's why she doubted I'd be successful." I wanted to add that she had taken my $1000 before telling me this; but I had made a vow to be kind to Laura while I was being angry with the rest of the world.

"I'll call the director," said Laura. "Her name is Donna. I don't think she'd hide anything from us."

The next day I returned home from work to find a message on my answering machine from Laura. "Good news from Rainbow House! They have two little Russian boys and single men are okay. I'm away overnight. Call me in the morning!"

I dropped to my knees and stroked the answering machine like a beloved pet. "Single men are okay." It was like hearing one of the beatitudes Christ had forgotten to mention in his Sermon on the Mount: "Blessed are the single men, and they shall get their share of children from Russian orphanages." Now I had to wait until morning to find out about these two Russian boys. I wondered how many other couples and singles between Maine and New Mexico were competing for them. It was hopeless . . . hopeless. But no, it was not hopeless or else Laura would not have asked me to call her in the morning. I didn't know what to think anymore. I was able to concentrate only when I called Marilyn to mind. My anger with her had a purifying effect on my thoughts and perhaps a conjuring effect on events as well, for that same evening Marilyn called. Jorge had resurfaced.

"He has no leads for you on a Guatemalan child yet," she said, as if we were back to business as usual and bygones were, once again, bygones.

"Wait a minute, Marilyn," I counseled. "Back up. Where was he?"

"Who?"

"Jorge."

"Oh, he was away."

"And he thinks it appropriate to leave his clients thinking that he's absconded with our money?"

Marilyn became defensive, but I welcomed this show of honest emotion. It represented the bedrock of who she really was, beyond which there could be no obfuscation. "Listen, I don't control him," she said. "That's just the way he is."

I struck back immediately. "It's no way to do business," I said. "It's no way to treat people who are relying on you for something this important."

"Anyway," said Marilyn, unwilling to go head to head on the issue, "you'll need to do some forms over."

"But I thought I had all my forms in."

"Yes, but the Guatemalan courts have changed the format on some of them. I'll send them along as soon as I can."

"When will that be?"

"As soon as I can. God, this neighborhood has had it. I don't dare go out at night."

April 1, 1993. I got out of bed at the break of dawn. I would say "woke up," but I had not slept. I felt as if I had been floating above my bed, barely in contact with the sheets, held aloft by the kinetic energy of my apprehensions.

I called Laura at 8:00 A.M.. She told me she had spoken with the director of Rainbow House, Donna Clauss. "Donna does not hold Marilyn in high regard," was her first comment.

"So you told her I've been working with Marilyn?"

"I told her everything about you. I think I read half your homestudy over the phone."

"Laura," I begged. "Do you have any news for me?" I was pressing my palmprint into the receiver.

"Here's the story," began Laura. "There is currently a moratorium on Russian adoptions."

My heart sank. "Is the moratorium on the part of the Russians or the Americans?" I interrupted.

"The Russians." Laura paused, sensed that I had nothing else to say at the moment, and went on. "But children approved for adoption prior to December 15 can still be matched."

My spirits soared. "What about the two boys?" I pressed.

"They fall into this category."

"Which category?" I was not thinking again, just reflexing.

"Preapproval. They're cleared to go."

They're cleared to go! "Go on, Laura."

"One is named Misha. He's almost five. Blond with blue eyes. He's supposed to have had surgery for a clubbed left foot, but Donna says his foot looks fine."

Misha Klose, I thought. It sounded like Russian fast food. "What about the other boy?"

"He's a bit older," said Laura. "His name's Alyosha. He's six going on seven. Donna describes him as sweet, bright, normal, and healthy. Both boys are in orphanages in the city of Tula, south of Moscow."

Six going on seven moved beyond what I had set as my upper age limit. Then I caught myself: There were no more hard-and-fast age limits. There was only a need to adopt one of these boys.

"Can I get photos?" I asked, although I was now willing to submit to the Kerry treatment and forego pictures. I realized I was on emotional afterburners. Failing this, I would have no more to give.

"Donna says she has a video of Alyosha and a picture of Misha."

A video! Above and beyond the call of duty.

"Give her a call," said Laura. "This one looks very good. I think it's going to work."

I almost hung up on Laura in my eagerness to contact Donna. I dialed through and got her on the third ring. "I thought you'd be calling!" she exclaimed.

"Should I start telling you my life's story?"

"No need," said Donna. "Laura told me everything and I trust her completely. Did she tell you I have a video of Alyosha? . . ."

"And a photo of Misha," I said, completing her sentence. "When can I see them?"

"Tomorrow," she said. "I'll FedEx them to you today."

My head was spinning off my shoulders. I could not believe how quickly everything was happening. My contact with Rainbow House was only days old and already I was receiving pictures of my future son—my future son! Either Misha or Alyosha, I was sure of it. Then I commanded myself not to be sure of anything. But I knew enough to be grateful that I was (at last!) speaking with someone who was giving me the benefit of any possible doubt and a video to boot.

"What are your feelings about my possibilities?" I asked.

"I think you may be able to fly to Russia in May."

Next month! Could Donna really make it happen that quickly? "Donna," I confided, "after all I've been through I feel almost obligated to be skeptical."

Donna laughed. "I'll call Moscow again today to double-check on the two boys."

"And they're cleared for adoption by a single man?" I said, my mouth closing about the last word, as if this was the question I dared not ask for fear of corrupting the entire process.

"That's my understanding," said Donna. "But I'll ask again."

I almost did not want her to ask again. I wanted to go to Moscow on hearsay, hoping that upon seeing me the Russians would be too embarrassed to send me back empty-handed. I asked Donna about the dossier for her Russian program.

"Birth certificate, employer letter, proof of health insurance . . ." she recited. The list was shorter than that for Marilyn's Guatemala program. "You already have a completed homestudy and reference letters, which Laura is sending me. And Laura makes you sound like the perfect dad for one of these kids."

Dad, another new word appended to me. "Donna," I asked, "have you done a Russian adoption for a single man before?" This was an important question. Even professionals were prone to falsely elevating their clients' hopes at times.

Donna sighed. "We had one case," she said, "which didn't work out well, so this is a good question you're asking. The short answer is no, we've never completed an adoption on a single man in this program."

She went on to relate the story of a man in New Mexico who had been matched with a little boy in Russian Karelia, near the Finnish border. "He had a picture of this little boy, he had fallen in love with him, writing him letters, preparing his room. . . ."

I swallowed hard for both of us. "And?"

"And at the last minute they just said no."

"They?"

"The adoption authorities in Russia."

"Why?"

"We never found out. It's not easy to get answers out of them. And you can't make demands the way you can here. There's the danger of jeopardizing the whole program."

I thought hard for a moment. "What happened with the prospective father?"

Donna sighed again. "He went into an absolute tailspin. It was terrible. He was heartbroken and we still can't get him to look at another child. This man would have been the first single male for us. So if we can get you one of these boys you'll be making history."

This was a challenge I didn't need at the moment. I did not want to be epoch making. I simply wanted to slip in, get my son, and slip out. Things could wax momentous once I had landed in New York. "I'll be anxious to hear what Moscow says," I told Donna. "Is there anything else I can do in the meantime?"

"Are you involved with any other programs?" she asked. "Oh, that's right. Laura said you're working with Marilyn."

"I'm not sure that I am. But I hear that you've had something to do with her in the past. What can you tell me?"

Donna did not mince her words, and I respected her for this. "She promised us children she was unable to deliver," she said. "This put us in some very difficult situations with adoptive parents. We just won't work with her anymore."

"Donna," I said, "Laura probably told you that Marilyn and her Guatemalan contact have my money but there is no evidence of any child yet."

Donna sympathized with me. "We do require that if you submit an application to us you withdraw any applications you have with other adoption sources. This is to protect the children."

"Donna," I said, "if you call me after speaking with Moscow and tell me that I can adopt either Alyosha or Misha, I will work with you exclusively and without reservation. I won't have any problem terminating my relationship with Marilyn. In the meantime, what else can I do while waiting to hear from you?"

"Just wait for the video," she said.

After two years of waiting I could endure another twenty-four hours.

But I would have to choose between Misha and Alyosha. I already felt myself leaning toward Misha because of his age. How could I approach the two with an even hand? Did I really have to? Something in one of these boys would speak to me in some special, unequivocal way. I was convinced of this, and it was something I should not be intimidated by; I should be luxuriating in it. Where yesterday there was famine, today I was being served an embarrassment of delicacies.

Tomorrow I would see my son for the first time.

Gift from the East

The idea that Misha's and Alyosha's pictures were winging their way toward me before Donna had double-checked with Russia gave me reason to pause and worry a bit. What if I fell in love with one or both of these boys and Russia said no? I had read in an adoption book that it is impossible to fall in love with someone you do not even know. I could not agree with this and wound up pitying the author of that thought. The eye gathers so much more than surfaces. It sees deeply, it sets images in motion. I considered myself to have a discerning eye for character and personality. I had no doubt that the moment I saw the images of these Russian boys, a process of calculation would begin in my head, highly seasoned with imagination, of course, but leading nonetheless to my full-hearted dedication to one of them. At least I hoped that one would speak louder than the other. I had fallen into the habit of mentally reciting their names as Misha and Alyosha, but never Alyosha and Misha. Did this point to a subconscious preference for Misha? If so, why? Because Laura had mentioned his name first? Because he fell into the age range I was looking for? Because I felt that a younger child would more readily accept me?

The second of April dawned with a soft brilliance that laid itself out along a diaphanous cloud cover on the eastern horizon. The sky was apricot and the air was fresh, fresh with the wet earth smell of early spring. It was a Friday and I had to go to the university to teach. On the one hand, it seemed irreverent to do anything other than wait for the FedEx truck to arrive. I mean, this was the stork coming to alight on my chimney. On the other hand, I was grateful to have such an all-encompassing distraction as teaching biology to forty undergraduates. My involvement with them always made kindling out of my days: a quick fire, soon over. Yes, the time would pass.

I had always felt a special relationship to my students, seeing them as mine and nobody else's. At some level, I am sure I believed that when they walked out of my classroom they had nothing else to do but wait in anxious anticipation for my next lecture. But in recent years I had made more of an attempt to conduct the business of teaching without martyring myself for the cause. Maybe I was just getting older and had less and less in common with my students as the years wore on. But on this day as I stood before them, I made an effort to look at every earnest (if not eager) face, as if bidding each of them good-bye for the last time. I felt it in my bones that I would soon be the father of one of the two Russian boys being sent to me in a self-sealing envelope. Once I had given myself over heart and soul to the adoption of that child, a new and clearer boundary would appear in my life: *Your students are not your friends or your family. They are the people you teach.*

As I stood in front of the classroom lecturing on the structure of DNA, I found that I could not take my mind off the FedEx truck. I kept glancing at the clock on the back wall with all the anticipation of my most long-suffering biology students. My gosh, I thought, I have to get home or at least get to a phone and tell FedEx to leave the package on my doorstep. No, then someone might steal it. What am I talking about? This is Maine. Nobody would steal it.

After my lecture I was the first one out of the room. I made my call. No delivery had been made yet. My two little comrades were still bouncing along the road in the FedEx truck. I gave instructions to leave the delivery at the door if they got there before I did. I hopped into my pickup and headed for home. The day had become even more beautiful as it matured. Upon arriving I snuck around to my back porch and felt my heart race as I considered that the envelope might already be there.

No. Nothing. I went inside and checked the answering machine. No messages. It was 2:00 P.M.. FedEx did not deliver past 6:00, right? That meant within the next four hours I would *know*.

But I was not given that much time. At 3:15 the truck pulled up and the young driver bounced out, swinging a large white envelope by its corner. He eyed me and then felt through the envelope. "Ah, a video," he said, and then he winked at me. He looked at the return address. "Rainbow House. They all have those kinds of names. Fantasy this, Dream that."

I was glad these guys did not warrant tips, because I would not have given him one. "It's not what you think," I said, signing my name and taking the envelope from him. My next impulse was to explain what exactly it was, but I quelled this urge and took my business inside.

I opened the envelope carefully, pulling the sticky flap from one side to the other. Then I reached inside and removed a plastic video case, cracked it open, and beheld the tape. I did not have a VCR, but my friend Mary, of sticky-bun fame, did. I called her immediately. The phone rang without result. Damn. I called another friend—no answer there either. "Where are these people!" I said aloud. I checked my watch. It was not even 3:30. Oh, they're working.

I considered going up to the university library to play it on one of the units available for general use. But these were on desktops in public view, and I felt this to be one of the most private things I had ever done. I wanted surroundings where I could react as I needed to.

I sat down at the kitchen table and balanced the tape on my palm. The label said "Alyosha." Then I thought of Misha. Donna had said she would be sending a picture. I dug back into the FedEx envelope—no Misha. She must have forgotten. So I had only one of the boys, the one, truth to tell, I was not anticipating being smitten with as much as the other. Still, I was champing at the bit, anxious to see Alyosha, eager to know if my perceptions approached Donna's representation of this boy.

Mary got home at exactly 5:00 P.M. I know this because I had been calling her every five minutes since 3:30. "Where have you been?" I asked, putting a last-minute lilt on the statement only after most of it had left my mouth. But I think it still came out as chastisement. Didn't Mary know that my life was at stake?

"Working," she said. "What about you?"

"Languishing," I said, and then I mentioned the video.

"You come right over here!" she ordered. "Now!"

I was airborne, exceeding every posted speed limit, disgusted with the slowness of other drivers and the unhurried pace of pedestrians, and yet I would love them all if only they would get out of my way!

Ten minutes later I pulled up in front of Mary's. Her two young children were there as well. They had been informed of the gravity of the moment and dutifully took their places on the sofa, waiting patiently for the show to begin.

"You want something to drink?" asked Mary.

"Maybe *after* the video," I said, though she was proffering only orange juice.

I pulled up a chair directly in front of the television, at a decidedly unsafe distance. And there I sat and there I peered while Mary pushed "play" and the first dead inches of the tape slipped through the machine.

Some snow, a flash of light, two figures mired in shadows, everything out of focus, and then the images spun out of control, as if the person holding the camera was swinging it about his head. More shadows, light streaming through a curtain, a Russian chest of drawers, a tile floor. . . .

"There he is!" I shouted, pointing to the screen. Mary and the children leaned closer in. A little black-haired boy with a dark complexion; that could not be him. Alyosha was supposed to be blond. Is this a mistake? Or was the descriptive information simply incorrect? No. Wait! The little black-haired boy slipped onto a chair next to a little blond-haired boy. Both of them were smacking away on bubble gum, and then the camera settled on the blond-haired boy.

"This is Alyosha, yes?" said a woman. I recognized it as Donna's voice.

I became fully unaware of anyone else being in the room with me. Yet my blood did not rush, my heart did not leap. I simply felt that I wanted to be alone with this child and see and hear all that he had to offer me. He was wearing a Mickey Mouse sweatshirt that showed Mickey from behind. The caption read, "Mickey's Back!" The red dye had run from the sleeves. He also had on black-and-white checked pants, Russian sneakers, and a collared shirt under the sweatshirt. It occurred to me that these were probably his best clothes.

Through a translator Donna asked Alyosha if he would like to have a family in America. *"Da,"* he said in a small, reedy voice. Then he smiled: a broad, sunny smile that made almond slivers of his narrow, wide-set eyes. "Is there anything you recite?" she asked. *"Da,"* he said again. I quickly learned to love this word, maybe because it sounded so much like "Pa."

Alyosha stood up with a bit of reluctance. He dropped his hands to his sides and began to recite a poem. From memory. Iambic pentameter. Singsong. As his piece appeared to draw to a close, the women applauded and sang out, *"Kharashó!"* ("Very good!"). But Alyosha preempted them and resumed his piece. He had paused only to catch his breath. The women fell silent and waited respectfully for him to finish. A few moments later he uttered his last syllables and they cheered him anew.

A poet, I thought. What more could I ask for? A poet from the land of Pushkin.

Alyosha looked into the lens of the video camera as Donna launched a few more questions at him. I leaned in toward the screen and actually felt closer to him—those eyes, that impish twinkle, that demure expression.

"What do you like to do?" asked Donna. Alyosha answered and I waited for the translation. "Play with the big boys," he said. "And he wants to have a family in America?" Donna asked again.

"Da."

Then, nothing. The tape blacked out. It had lasted about four minutes. "Should I play it again?" asked Mary. I nodded. I wanted to see it again, but probably not a third time. The dose had become of paramount importance now, for it had happened. My eye had perceived all that was perceivable. The calculations had been made. Yes, I wanted to see the tape again, but I was already in love with Alyosha. Yet experience had taught me that his adoption could not yet be presumed. Therefore an addictive cycle of viewing and reviewing the tape ran the risk of setting me up for devastating disappointment. My lack of a playback unit made it easier for me to abstain.

On the way home I thought of Misha. I realized that it was providence that I had seen Alyosha first. I would still look at Misha's picture, because I had told Donna that I would. But I had already made up my mind to ask to adopt Alyosha, convinced that there was nothing in another child's picture that could wean me away from him. It was like parents in a schoolyard; they did not look at other children and wish they had them instead of their own. At least I didn't think they did.

The next day I called Donna. "I've seen Alyosha's video."

"And?"

"And he's perfect for me," I said.

"I forgot to put Misha's picture in the envelope," she apologized. "But I sent it out today. So you'll still be able to see both boys. Call me back as soon as you can."

Two days later Misha's picture arrived. He was sweet, a good-looking little Russian boy, his blond hair in ringlets over his forehead. There was only one thing. He was not my boy. I felt as if a friend had sent me a photo of his kid and I was dutifully warmed by the child's aspect. But I did not want him to live with me. I waited an appropriate number of hours before seizing the phone and calling Rainbow House.

"Donna," I said, "I would really like to adopt Alyosha. I might have felt differently had Misha's picture gotten here first and he had had the chance to get under my skin, but I don't think so. I know my own mind in this."

Donna was clearly happy for me. "I think Alyosha's perfect for you, too."

Then I broached the crucial question. "Donna, can I consider Alyosha to be my referral?"

"Yes, you can. I'll send you the paperwork on him right away, along with our agency agreement."

"I can't believe this is happening," I confided. And then, apprehensively, "What did Moscow say?"

Donna had gotten through to them the day before. "Everything's fine," she said. "Alyosha could use a dad."

All further speech seemed superfluous. I was in Donna's hands and grateful for it.

"There's one other thing I'll need," she said.

"What's that?"

"A statement that you're, quote, free of pathological psychological disorders. It can be from a doctor, a school counselor, anybody qualified to make this assessment. This will make the Russians happy."

I suddenly realized I would do anything to make the Russians happy, even tell them what kind of tree I would like to be.

That night I sank into bed and covered my face with my hands. I realized that if I had begun with Rainbow House in the first place the whole adoption would probably have happened in less than a year. I could not believe how quickly things were developing or how consistently reliable Donna was proving to be. Why was she working so hard to match me with a Russian child any couple would give the world to adopt? I had no intention of asking her this question. I had no intention of looking a gift horse in the mouth, if indeed that is what this was.

And then there was Marilyn. I lugged my body out of bed and trudged over to the phone. Even thinking of Marilyn was becoming painful. There was no answer at her end. I tried again a bit later in the evening. Nothing. Perhaps she had flown the coop to divvy up the loot with Jorge.

Having failed to reach Marilyn, it occurred to me that I had to call Laura and tell her my good fortune. When she answered I told her right off that I was a sucker for Alyosha. Realizing how repetitive I was coming to sound, I still could not keep from telling her, "He's perfect for me."

Laura was all ears, drinking in all of my impressions and making notes at her end of the line. "When will you travel?" she asked.

"Donna said something about May."

"Unbelievable. Are you ready?"

"I want this with all my heart."

Over the next several days I continued to dial Marilyn's number, growing more certain with every failed attempt that she was gone for good. It took Herculean force of will to give her the benefit of the doubt and consider that she might simply be on vacation. But if that were the case, why hadn't she told me? I wanted to tell her personally of my decision to adopt Alyosha, but I finally decided to leave a message to this effect. "And I'd like a refund of the money I sent Jorge," I added, not even mentioning the $1000 I had sent her.

A few days later I returned home to a message on my answering machine. Marilyn. Surprisingly, she was cheerful and supportive. I stared down at the answering machine as her grating voice clawed out at me. "Good for you," she said. "You're doing the right thing. If I were you I'd stop payment on the checks you sent Jorge. Talk to you later."

I had not thought of stopping payment, probably because it did not seem worth considering. I had sent the money to Jorge months before and was sure he had cashed the money orders by now, but I had nothing to lose. So I took Marilyn's advice, contacted the bank, and read them the serial numbers over the phone. After consulting with their computers for a minute or two the answer came back: the money orders had long ago been cashed.

I considered forgetting the $3000 I had sent Jorge, rationalizing that in risking an adoption with him he had unknowingly driven me into the arms of Rainbow House and my prospective son. But I was not built for that kind of forgiveness. In my mind the world worked as well as it did because account ledgers balanced: I wrote a check, you cashed it, you delivered the goods. But with Jorge this rule had been violated and the imbalance weighed heavily on my soul, as if I would be letting the world down if I did not do everything possible to set the ledger straight.

A couple of days later I received a call from Marilyn. She congratulated me again on my good fortune. As for Jorge: "Write him a letter," she advised. "Send me a copy and in a couple of weeks I'll contact him."

"Why a couple of weeks?"

"I need time," was her enigmatic reply.

I dutifully wrote the letter, made a copy for Marilyn, and mailed it. The language was diplomatic but unequivocal. I thanked Jorge for his efforts but requested a refund, telling him he could deduct what he considered to be a fair fee for his work on my behalf.

Near the end of the month I drove down to my agency to show off the video of Alyosha to Laura. A couple of other caseworkers joined us in front of the television set. This was the first time I had seen the tape since the debut at Mary's house. Its effect on me was even more profound now, because the comments of Laura and the others made me swell with pride. They were talking about my boy.

"He looks wonderful," said Laura. "There's something about these Russian kids. Oh, Bob, I wouldn't hesitate if I were you."

"I'm not hesitating," I concurred. "This is the kid I want."

By the beginning of May I, once again, had assembled all of my documents for my dossier. I took the pile to the town hall to have them notarized, and then drove to Augusta for the apostilles. This time there were only eight documents. The next day I FedExed the dossier to Rainbow House.

In the middle of May I received the following placement agreement from Rainbow House:

> I, Robert Klose, do hereby accept the child, Alyosha, with a given date of birth of 5 September, 1985, presently residing in an orphanage in the Tula District, Russia, offered to me for adoptive placement through Rainbow House. I understand that Rainbow House International is not responsible for representations made of this child by the Ministry of Education, Moscow, Russia, or the orphanage in Tula, Russia, as their role is a limited one.

There it was, then: my name and Alyosha's together on the same page. The birth date caught my eye. Alyosha was not six, as I had been told. He was seven and rapidly approaching eight. But this issue was now moot. He was beautiful and he had stolen my heart and he was going to be mine.

A week later I touched base with Marilyn again. Her program had become the thorn in my side.

"Have you heard from Jorge?" she asked.

I told her no, and that I was growing impatient.

"Try calling him," she said.

"No," I shot back. "You try calling him. I gave you a thousand dollars. Now advocate for me." Through all of this, I resented the rancor I was continuing to feel. I did not want Alyosha to have an angry dad.

"I'll try," she said.

That same day I spoke with Donna. She had received my signed placement agreement, but travel during May seemed increasingly unlikely. Even to me it had seemed too optimistic. "I think you'll be going to Russia on June nineteenth," she said.

"That's pretty specific."

Donna explained that she tried to send adoptive parents over in groups. "Others will be traveling at the same time," she added. "So look into booking your flight now. Give yourself two weeks in Russia." Then she recommended her travel agent. "She's worked with many of our adoptive parents and knows what you're going through."

A couple of days later, however, Donna called back. "June nineteenth won't work," she said. "Book a departure on July second, arriving in Moscow on the third."

"Is this solid?" I asked.

"As solid as these things can be."

On June first I received a photo of Alyosha, taken in the orphanage by Americans who had been there some months before. He was wearing the same clothing, Mickey Mouse shirt and checked pants, but his expression was plain, almost unwitting, making me wonder if he knew what was going on. In the interim I had learned—from a Russian neighbor—that Alyosha is a diminutive or endearment of his given name, Alexei. Alexei Klose, a beautiful name.

I now settled down to the long business of waiting. All the phone calls had been made; all the documents had been signed, notarized, and apostilled; all the stars seemed to be sitting in their assigned places in the heavens.

But Alyosha was still little more than a twinkle in my eye.

I Am Bound Away

I called the travel agency Donna had recommended. It was in California, a state for which I was losing all affinity as time wore on. Ellen was extremely pleasant and routinely handled the travel needs of Donna's clients. But when I received her quotes, they were well above what I had anticipated. Having flown to Germany on several occasions for $500 to $600 roundtrip, I could not imagine that Moscow would be that much more. However, ticket prices have no basis in logic. Ellen told me that my roundtrip price would be $2200 and Alyosha's one-way $980: over $3000 just for travel. This was plainly unacceptable.

I immediately began to think of alternative ways to get to Moscow. Fly to Germany and take the train? No, that would make the return trip for Alyosha interminable. What about a humanitarian fare? "Only on Lufthansa," said Ellen. "And they're booked."

If I was cornered I would find the $3000 somewhere. But I was a frequent traveler to Europe and had learned never to take the first price quoted. There was always a cheaper ticket somewhere, and I intended to do everything possible to find it.

After calling travel agency after travel agency, all of which gave me stiff prices, I finally found an old newspaper clipping from a "bucket shop" or consolidator, an agency that sells discounted tickets bought in advance from the airlines. When I explained my situation to the agent, Lita, she went to work for me with dedicated care. For the next four days we stayed in touch, until she was finally able to come up with an offer I could not refuse. "I've found tickets on Aeroflot," she said. "Eight hundred forty-five for you . . ."

"That's roundtrip?" I confirmed.

"Right."

"Beautiful. And what about Alyosha?"

"Two hundred."

"You're kidding!"

Lita had done it. She had saved me $2000. I told her to book the flights. Throughout the adoption process I had been looking for someone who would take mercy on me, and now I had found her. She had gotten me rock-bottom prices when she could easily have tried to sell me more expensive tickets. "There's one caveat," she said. "These are nonchangeable tickets. You must travel on July second and leave Russia on the eighteenth."

I was willing to agree to anything for the ticket price she had gotten me. At worst I saw myself staying beyond the eighteenth, losing the return flights, and having to take the train to Germany and fly out much more cheaply from there. But I also had another worry: would Donna call again with yet another departure date? If so, I would lose money even before I had taken off.

In the middle of June Donna did call, but regarding an entirely different, unanticipated matter. "I've received a fax from Russia," she sighed.

"Oh, no," I muttered. "It sounds like a problem."

"Not really," she said. "Just an unexpected formality."

"Formality?"

"One of the Russian adoption inspectors noticed that you're not married."

"Are you telling me I have to get married?"

"No," she laughed. "But this inspector does want a letter stating that you will eventually marry and that your wife will adopt Alyosha as well."

"Donna," I said, "I'll say anything I have to at this point."

"Okay, but I'll need the name of the prospective bride as well."

I thought hard for both of us. When would this trial end? I did not dare give the name of one of my female acquaintances here. Who knows what type of complications that might cause later? But beyond this, I had a hard time lying about someone who lived in my relative vicinity. Then it struck me—I knew a Danish woman. I could give the Russians her name. Somehow, the idea of having an ocean interposed between us made a lie more palatable, as if this woman lived in a different dimension where lies might not matter.

"Donna," I said. "Kirstine. Kirstine Hansen."

"Sounds Scandinavian," said Donna as she scribbled on the other end.

"She's Danish," I said.

"What does she do?"

"Actually, she's studying for the ministry in Copenhagen."

"Interesting!" said Donna. "Then I'll say that you intend to marry her and that she will adopt Alyosha; but that you want the adoption to be your first commitment before you enter into the marriage."

I winced as Donna recited this statement to me. All I could eke out was a modest, plaintive, "Yes." What a tangled web I was weaving.

"We're still waiting for your invitation," said Donna, moving on to the next topic.

"Invitation?"

"Yes, all travelers to Russia must have a formal invitation. Yours will come from the Ministry of Education. You can't even apply for your visa until it's arrived at the Russian consulate here."

"Donna," I said, "I leave in two weeks."

"Don't worry," she assured me. "The Russians have a habit of waiting until the last minute."

That same day my air tickets arrived in the mail. I was unable to rejoice in them because the issue of the invitation was weighing so heavily on my mind. How could the airline sell me tickets, I wondered, if there was no requisite invitation to travel to my destination?

Three days later, on June 22, Donna called. "We have your invitation!" she said. "Send for your visa."

The letter detailing my impending marriage to a lovely blond Dane in Copenhagen must have done the trick. As I hightailed it down to have my visa photos taken, I considered that someday I would tell Kirstine how much she had helped me in the adoption of my son. Yes, I would tell her... in about twenty years.

While all this was going on I had been trying on and off to reach Jorge in Guatemala. Marilyn had called me once. "Have you had any luck?" she asked through a rain of interference on the line, as if she were shouting through a brass pipe on the high seas.

"No," I told her. "Have you?"

She said she had not even been trying. "I just can't believe that guy," she clucked, as if Jorge were some mischievous teenager.

"I can, Marilyn," I told her. "He's taken my three thousand dollars and blown town."

"How's your Russian adoption going?" she asked, oblivious to my estimation of her business partner.

I told her I was leaving July 2, and then I chastised myself for carrying on a normal conversation with someone who had brought me to the brink of bankruptcy.

"Incredible," she said. "Listen. When you call Jorge again, ring once, hang up, and then phone again, but let the phone ring the second time."

"What are you talking about?"

"Maybe he has a system," she suggested. "You know, a signal he uses with his friends."

I actually paused to consider this scheme. I told Marilyn I would try it. "Let me know if it works," she said gamely.

It did not work. Over the next several days I continued to try getting through, returning to the traditional means of calling by letting the phone ring through on the first attempt. Then, one night, somebody answered. I was so surprised by this that I momentarily forgot where and whom I was calling. The male voice at the other end was patiently inquiring after the name of the caller. I finally responded in Spanish. "Yes, yes," Jorge said. "How is it going?"

How is it going? I bit the bullet. "Did you receive my letter?" I asked him, calmly, businesslike.

"Yes, yes," he said, switching over to impeccable English. "I am sorry not to have gotten back to you sooner."

Sooner. Hell, he had not gotten back to me at all. I found myself scrambling for the high ground. "Thank you again for all your work on my behalf," I said. "But you understand that I am leaving for Russia soon and..."

"When?" he asked, with passionate interest.

"On July second."

"Oh, I am so happy for you," he said. "I want to congratulate you."

The realization that this call was on my dime pushed me to raise the issue of my money at the first opportunity.

"Yes, yes," said Jorge. "Of course I will give you a refund. Do you want your papers back, too?"

I could not believe what I was hearing. I had prepared myself for some sort of resistance or defiance. But here he was, forthcoming, lucid, and encouraging. "Yes," I said. "if you could send my papers I'd appreciate it." Then a thought struck me: be magnanimous. "Jorge," I said. "I feel that you should receive something for the work you did for me, so I'd like you to deduct legitimate expenses."

"Yes," he said. "That would come to about four hundred dollars."

I thought this figure reasonable. His being so specific also struck me as a sign that he did, indeed, consider it his obligation to be fair. I was genuinely relieved and flattered by his cooperation, because at root I recognized that if he were to decide to keep all of the money there was probably nothing I could do about it.

"It will take me a couple of weeks to send you the money, though," he said. "I have to wait until my new clients pay me so I can pay you."

I told him that was acceptable, but that he should wait four weeks, until my return from Russia. He agreed. After a few more civil words we parted amicably. In my joy at what I considered to be a coup of sorts, I called Laura and told her of my good fortune. Her response was brief. "Oh, really? Well, we'll see."

I had my flight tickets, my invitation, and the visa was in the works. Barring my untimely death, I would be on a plane to Moscow in only a few days. I felt certain enough about my ultimate success to call the local grammar school and tell them to prepare for a little Russian boy.

"What grade will he enter?" asked the secretary.

What a matter-of-fact question, I thought. Why wasn't she hysterical with joy? I mean, this was my son we were talking about, and he's a Russian! Then I realized that I had given no thought to his grade placement. I must have thought that the school would simply put him where he belonged. I thought hard for a moment. He would be seven on arrival, but eight in September. What grade were eight year olds in? "Second grade," I finally said.

"Will he need English-as-a-second-language instruction?"

Gee, she must be reading items from a form right in front of her, I thought. Also, I had not anticipated any of the questions. I was sure Alyosha did not speak any English. "Yes," I said, seeing as the service was available, although I believed that ESL sometimes hurt more than it helped, as a child's really useful language is learned from family and peers.

There were a few more questions, mostly about special needs and prior schooling. "Okay," the secretary concluded. "I'll alert the school."

She would "alert" the school—only in a small Maine town.

Now that the board of education had been put on red alert, the cat was out of the bag and I no longer had any reason to keep things to myself. My correspondence and phone contacts now carried the news that I was adopting. From Russia.

"What's new with you?" asked a close friend in Pennsylvania. "I've decided to adopt." An e-mail message came in from another friend in California. "What have you been up to?" he asked. I hit the "reply" key and typed

I'M ADOPTING A LITTLE BOY FROM RUSSIA.

I continued to type, dropping a line to all of my acquaintances from Iceland to Japan.

I'M GOING TO RUSSIA IN A FEW DAYS TO ADOPT A LITTLE BOY.

The responses began to pour in. They were uniformly supportive. I appreciated all the kind words, I reveled in the externalizing of my story. At last, after having gone through so much, after all the hurtful days, solitary nights, sleepless nights, dead ends, frustrating denials, I was finally able to once again be a friend to my friends and tell them what was going on in my life. I had no regrets about keeping things to myself for so long. In doing so I had spared friends and acquaintances the ordeal of associating with a madman.

Near the end of June I began to prepare for the trip with urgent deliberation. I mowed the lawn, transferred the houseplants to a friend's place, stopped the mail, and shut off the hot water heater. I cleaned the house with a painstaking care that stopped short of sterilization. The Russians were a clean people and I wanted my son to walk into a clean house. My visa arrived in plenty of time and I put the finishing touches on the photo album I was bringing with me to Russia: pictures of my home, the river, the neighborhood, my canoe, the university where I worked, and my parents and other family members in New Jersey. So that Alyosha could have a preview of the life he would be entering. Last, but not least, I went to a local department store and bought a teddy bear.

June 30 was hot and clear, not the best driving weather for the ten-hour trip to New Jersey, where I would leave my truck with family before flying out of New York. Then again, climate was the least of my concerns.

After almost twenty-eight months of work, I was on the threshold of the most important step I had ever taken in my life. As I opened the door to my pickup I took a long look at my home. My eyes wandered over the white clapboards and black shutters to the backyard with its apple trees, the Cortlands just swelling on the dark branches. Beyond these trees the lawn dropped off to the river, which wandered south from this beautiful north country. When I returned, the first raspberries would be ripe for picking and the bass fishing would still be good. There was not enough to keep me here now, but so much to come back to. When I did return, I would set my little son loose in this world. Whatever he wanted to do I would let him do. There was nothing here that could hurt him, only spaces unlimited in which to grow and play out his every fantasy.

Even as I started the car I found myself missing Alyosha's childhood. How quickly his time with me would pass. This is the place, I thought, where his toys would be strewn and where he would hunt for frogs and turtles. Then, one day, he would abandon his toys and this place and find his heart's delight elsewhere. I would adopt him and he would be mine, but I knew that I was only borrowing him for a time, as all parents borrow a share of their children's lives. The trick, then, was to make the moments count. I was convinced this was possible for me. Having lived through the last twenty-eight months, I was convinced that anything was possible.

I backed out of my driveway and threw the truck into first gear. I slipped into second and then picked up speed in third. By fourth gear I was on the state road, by fifth on the interstate. I felt as if I were flying, breaking free of a gravity that would only stunt my growth if I continued to live in it alone. Before I knew it I had driven twenty miles, then thirty. South of Bangor, pine forests stretched away into the surrounding hills. Above, a great blue heron floated down onto a marsh. Yes, I thought, this is a fine season to adopt a little boy.

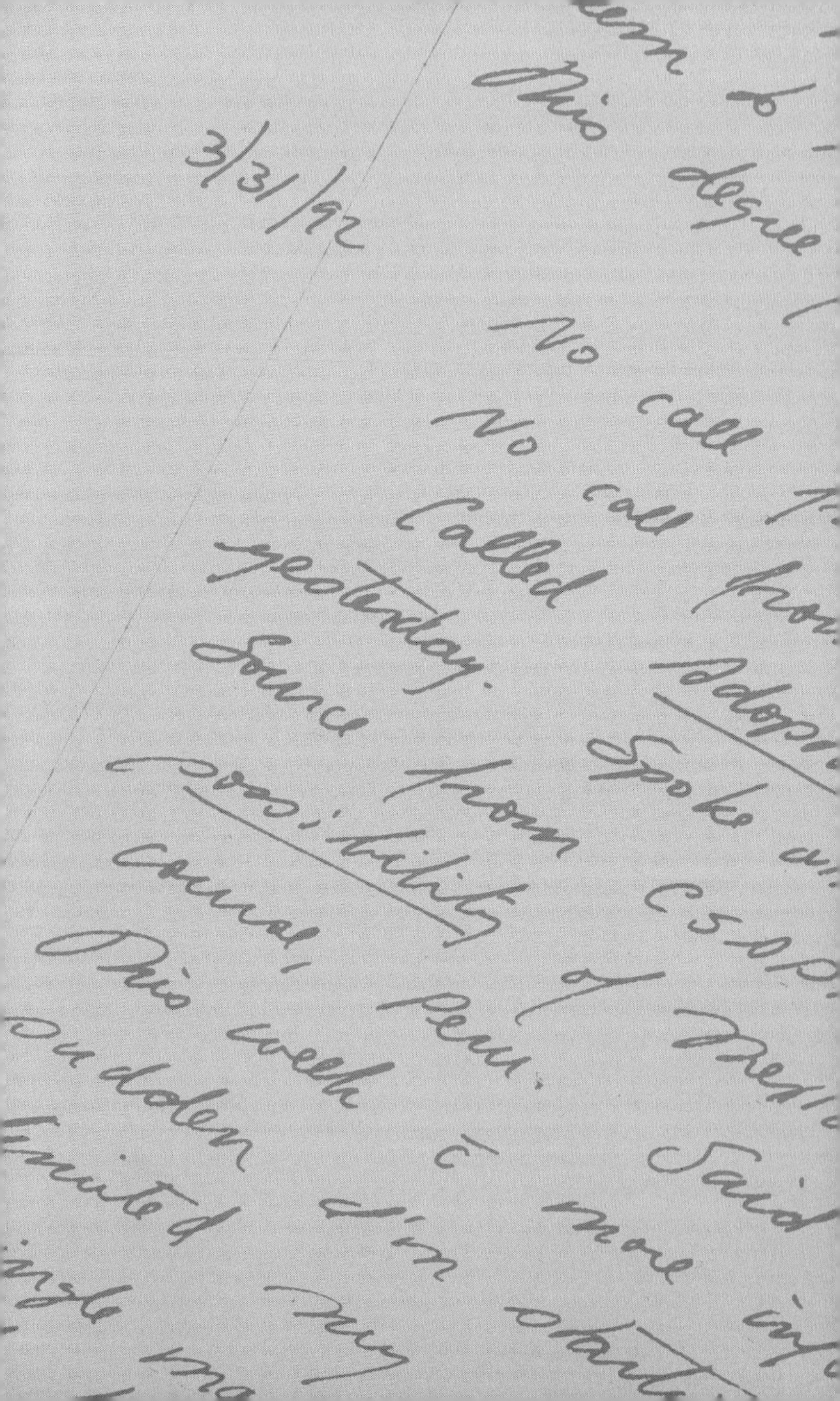

3/31/92

...em & ...
This degree (...

No call ...
No call from ...
Called Adopti...
yesterday. Spoke w...
Source from CSAP...
possibility of Mexi...
Conval. Peru. Said
This week c more inf...
On dozen c in...
invited ... start.
single ma...

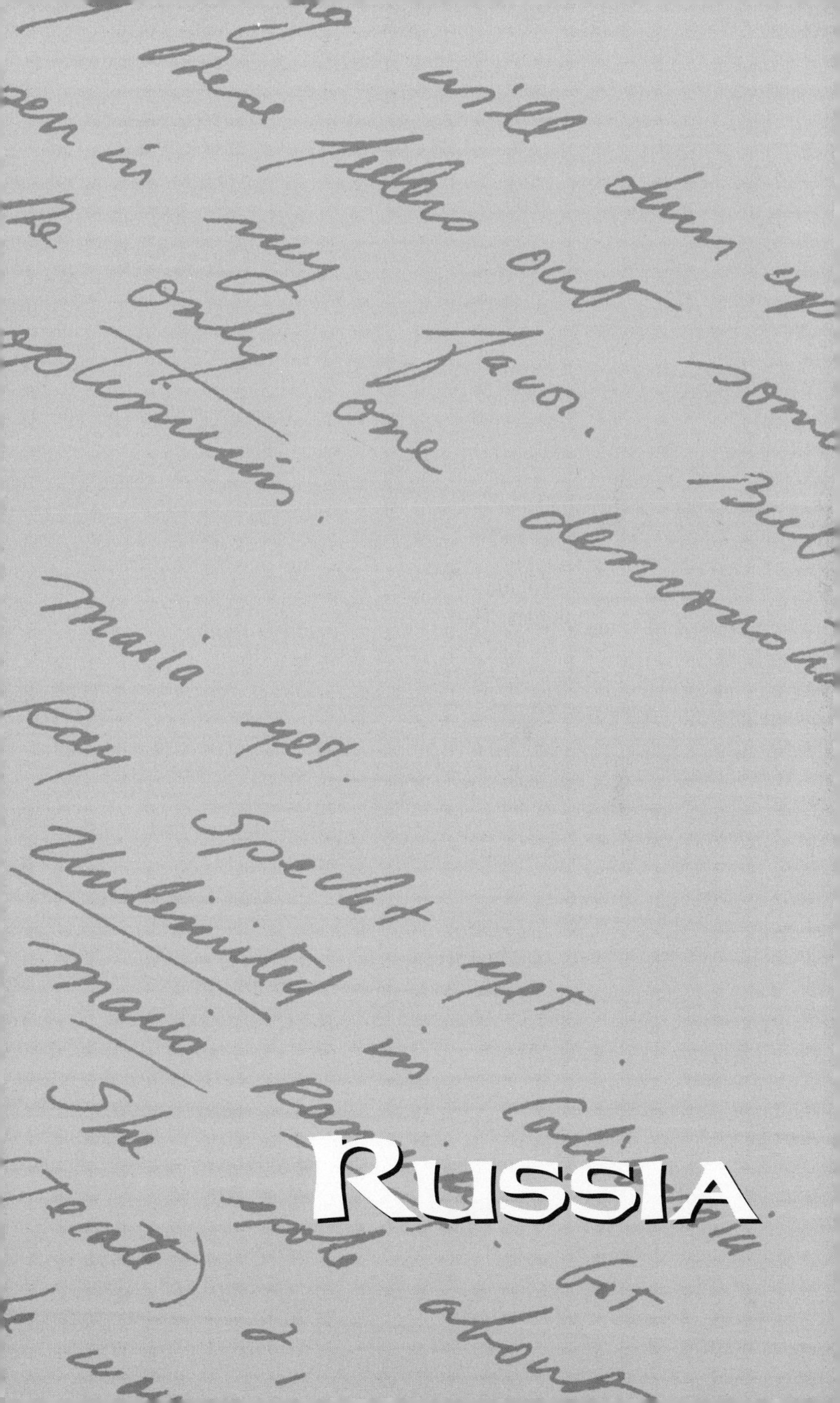

RUSSIA

Shuffling toward Moscow

I am in John F. Kennedy International Airport, waiting in line to check in for Aeroflot flight 316 to Moscow. All the other people in line are Russians. The men are thickset and sweating in dark, baggy suits. Their faces are wide enough to recline in. The women are caked with makeup and wearing oversized bracelets and earrings that jangle when they move.

Someone pushes me from behind, one of the thickset men. "Move up!" he barks. I comply.

Everyone is talking—the harsh palatalizations of the Russian language sound like water rushing past my ears. It is a breathless language. Perhaps the Russian bible reads, "In the beginning, there was the Paragraph."

I kick my Lands' End duffle along as the line inches forward. The Russians have no Lands' End duffles. They have no suitcases, no valises. They have cardboard boxes that are tied and taped to hold them together. I watch as an immense roll of duct tape is passed from hand to hand to reinforce the boxes that are bursting at the seams from being kicked along the floor as if they were Lands' End duffles. I consider this to be the last vestige of the old Soviet socialism: everyone is entitled to the roll of duct tape... except for me. When the duct tape reaches the man in front of me, he passes it over my head.

I find myself offended by these people. They look dangerous. They cast no shadows, because they are shadows. They look as if they could have their hands in my pocket at any moment, and yet my prospective son is Russian. In eighteen years will he be standing in an Aeroflot line in New York, smoking black tobacco, fingering a roll of duct tape, and filling a suit that could also serve as a double-breasted pup tent?

The adoption is not yet a done deal. It cannot even be presumed, even though I am traveling to Russia on the invitation of the adoption authorities there. I already know what my son looks like. Although I had steeled myself against it, when I saw his video I fell in love with him almost immediately. Now my heart is committed while my head tells me not to jump the gun. My task at the moment is not to pretend that Alyosha, age seven, is my son. My task is to kick my Lands' End duffle along the floor.

I have been standing in line for thirty minutes and have almost reached the ticket counter. Suddenly, six people come out of nowhere and pile in front of me. They push me back to make room for themselves. I stumble into a man who looks like Nikita Khrushchev. He pushes me forward. The people in front of me push me back. Several Russians somewhere else in the line shout their objections. Then the line calms, the conversations resume, and the duct tape continues its rounds.

During my parenting classes I had mentioned that I felt prepared for anything in my son's personality. Now I find myself hoping that he will not be a pusher.

I have been standing in line for forty-five minutes. The people who cut in front of me are now being waited on. I have to go to the bathroom—desperately. I turn to the man behind me, the one who looks like Khrushchev. Although he had pushed me earlier, he seems rather benign. He does not look as if he would take off his shoe and beat it on a table at the United Nations. "Do you speak English?" I ask him.

He takes the cigarette from his mouth. "*Da.*"

I ask him if he would be kind enough to watch my Lands' End duffle while I go to the bathroom.

"*Da.*"

I am gone ten minutes. When I return I notice that the line has advanced a tad and that the man who looks like Khrushchev has been kicking my Lands' End duffle along for me. I rejoin the line. "Thank you," I say.

He nods. "Why are you going to Russia?" he asks.

I am struck by his English, which is almost unaccented. I tell him that I am adopting a little Russian boy.

The man removes the cigarette from his mouth and puts that hand on my shoulder. I can feel the heat from the cigarette behind my ear. "Thank you," he says, "for adopting one of these children." Then he smiles at me, as if apologizing for his entire country.

The next thing I know he is handing me the roll of duct tape that he has just received from the woman behind him. "Pass it along," he says, and I hand the roll to the person in front of me.

I suddenly feel that I belong in this line, that I have been accepted into the circle of duct-tape passers.

"Next."

It is the ticket agent. I pick up my duffle, take one giant step forward, and then another.

Aboard Aeroflot Flight 316

5:03 P.M.

Although we have seat numbers on our boarding passes, there is no ordered seating by rows. Instead, the attendant simply tells the immense waiting-room crowd to get on the plane.

The rush aboard is like being part of the Oklahoma land grab. Bodies, bodies, a sea of bodies washing aboard like a polyester tsunami. When I finally find my seat I collapse into it for safety's sake, if nothing else, while a wave of humanity washes past me down the aisle. A man with a box slung to his back spins about and wallops me in the side of the head. Two women pause to back their buttocks into my face. The seat back in front of me cannot be raised—it is flopped down into my lap. I try to fix it in the midst of all this commotion, but I cannot, so I resign myself to the inconvenience. A passing Russian man tells me that I am in his seat, which means that mine is the recliner. I struggle to my feet and fight my way forward into the broken seat. Now I am the only passenger lying down. Worse, my seatbelt will not rewind. It is fully played out, suitable for restraining Moby Dick. So I lie here, feeling like an apparition floating on the vapors of vodka that fill the plane, dwelling on my cheap tickets, and not on the fact that Aeroflot has a reputation for crashing into mountainsides.

6:00 P.M.

The plane is still on the ground. The compartment is inexcusably hot, the aisles still packed with bodies. But no one else seems to be disturbed by the delay or the heat. Most of the Russians are collapsed into rumpled heaps in their seats. Shoeless, they eat hard-boiled eggs and drink from thermoses, conversing resignedly while I lie in repose. The food has made me hungry, but I am unwilling to rise from my bier and push Russians aside to get a bite for myself. It seems enough for the moment to stare upward and dream of the apple in my carry-on bag in the overhead compartment, hovering above me like an icon. It will reward my patience.

6:10 P.M.

The plane is moving! But people are still walking up and down the aisles as if on a bus. A female flight attendant with the build of a mud wrestler heads down the aisle at high speed. She trips on the torn carpet and is launched headlong into my lap. She pushes herself away from me and back onto her feet, straightening her flight cap with annoyance. Then she is gone.

7:00 P.M.

The plane is still on the ground, but we are in line for takeoff. The stewardess announces that we will be making two stops — in Gander, Newfoundland, and Shannon, Ireland. Five minutes later the captain announces that this is a nonstop flight. Then the dark man sitting next to me leans over and confides that we are going to a place called Omsk. I think he must be joking. I search his face for signs of laughter, but he does not move a facial muscle and falls back into his seat.

The plane is infested with American evangelists. They are all from Dixie and are ostensibly headed to redeem Russia. They wear tags with the names of their organizations; the one I am able to read is "Milk and Honey." They are mostly middle aged and seemingly well heeled. Many have their children along; the boys have short, pomaded hair, the girls wear cotton dresses. The evangelists keep getting up to stretch and to complain. They are all complaining.

One portly man, who is about fifty with a silver mane, complains that he should be given a hot facial towel. The woman sitting near him asks him what he expects from the Russians. "They're a real mess," she says. "You can't expect service from them." Then she exclaims, "Praise the Lord!" and says that she is happy to be going to do God's work in Russia, even if it does mean hardship for her. To this the man replies, with less gusto, "Praise the Lord," as if he were saying "You're welcome."

A man who looks like Errol Flynn gets up and says, "This plane makes me sick." The same woman who had spoken to the man without the facial towel says, "Yes, Harlen, but you'll be given the strength to endure it, Praise the Lord." Harlen says "Amen" and sits back down.

Getting hit in the head with the Russian's box felt good compared to these conversations.

7:10 P.M.

Airborne! All the evangelists are applauding. The man beside me is repeating "Ohm" with his eyes closed, but I wonder if he is saying "Omsk." I have managed to force a folded newspaper into the angle of my seat, wedging it somewhat upright, but my seatbelt is still as flaccid as a noodle. I take comfort in knowing that if we crash, I will have no trouble getting out of my seat.

I reach under my seat for the teddy bear hanging out of my backpack. I scratch it behind the ears. Then I pull it up into my lap, unconsciously cuddling it while I rest my eyes. It is Alyosha's bear, but it is my charm. There is something to be said for charms. This one tells me that with each passing hour I draw closer to Russia, and that at this very minute my prospective son is sleeping in a warm bed in an orphanage one hundred miles to the south of Moscow. I open my eyes and look up to see the portly evangelist in need of a facial towel staring down at me. "Your teddy?" he asks.

I smile. "I never fly without it."

Praise the Lord.

On Aeroflot's Tenuous Wings

We have been airborne for two hours, my teddy and I. At long last a flight attendant comes by, pushing a cart, proffering soft drinks, wine, beer, and snacks. I ask for a Coke. "May I have some peanuts too?" I ask, pointing. The flight attendant shakes her head. She does not understand. "Peanuts," I repeat, louder.

"Penis?" she says.

I redden, shake my head, and bury my face in my drink.

The flight attendant moves on. She is followed by another woman with a carton of steaming, lemon-scented facial towels, which she distributes with tongs. I instinctively look in the direction of the big evangelist, but he is not in his seat. I take my towel and pass it over my face. It loses its heat almost immediately, but it refreshes me nonetheless.

The big evangelist returns to his seat. He notices balled-up and folded facial towels all over the plane. His expression is forlorn. "I didn't get one," he says. Followed by, "Gosh darn it." What he really wants to say is, "God damn it," only he cannot, because he is an evangelist.

The willow-limbed woman traveling with him perks up. "It's a mess," she says disgustedly. "Their whole country is a mess. How do you expect to get a facial towel out of such a messed-up country, Praise the Lord?"

The man is not mollified by her rationale. He grits his jaw. He watches as the woman swipes her face with her towel, sighing with pleasure. He signals to the flight attendant, who ignores him. She is busy offering the other passengers penis.

As I sip my Coke I decide, at the eleventh hour, to learn some Russian phrases so that I will not be tongue-tied when I meet my son. I reach into my pocket and pull out a Berlitz phrase book loaned to me by a Russian friend in Maine. The copyright is 1959. The frontispiece contains an enigmatic notation: "The sale of this book is permitted only in North and Central America to the Panamanian-Colombian border; the islands of the West Indies, except Martinique and Guadeloupe; and the Hawaiian Islands." The 1950s was a cautious age, I guess, when the sale of a Russian phrase book in Guadeloupe constituted a capital crime. I turn a few more pages and am confronted with the near-hieroglyphics of Russian cyrillic. It looks like a more decorous version of the Roman alphabet or a jolly jumble of shapes and sizes from the mind's eye of a five year old. I search for phrases that might serve me in Russia: "Are those my shoes?" "I trust you had a satisfactory flight." "That's not the coffee. It's the tea." "My teeth are hurting me." "Are you a good boy?"

Oh, my. What if Alyosha is not a good boy? I hadn't thought of that. I quickly rummage around for the word "bad."

плохо

This looks like something a bad boy would write on a freshly painted wall.

Alyosha, what are my expectations of you? Before I left Maine, a Russian man told me that Russian children are less complicated to raise. But I cannot put stock in that, Alyosha. You will be growing up in America, not Russia. You will be coming into my life when you already have seven years of living experience behind you, with your own likes and dislikes, attitudes and ideas, patterns and spatial needs. You already know what makes you sad and what constitutes your delight. How do I work myself into a life that is already brimming with everything that fills it from day to day? How do you work yourself into mine?

I hope I can teach you something about myself and the place where I live and where both of us will make our home.

I think I am going to learn a lot from you, too.

Alyosha, be a good boy, and don't be a pusher.

We are landing in Gander, Newfoundland, after two and a half hours of flight. Word has spread among the evangelists that we are in Greenland.

The exodus from the plane is pell-mell, as if we had somewhere to go. People are bundling themselves, pulling bags from overheads, and pushing their sleepy children along. A Russian woman trips on the torn carpet next to me and then leers at me, as if I am the one responsible for the defect. I sit and wait until the floodwaters ebb. Then I get up, take my notebook, and mosey off the plane.

The night is softened by a full moon. As I walk away from the plane I pause to look back. It is immense, the biggest plane I have ever seen. I recall that Aeroflot's fleet, the largest in the world (2500 aircraft), is also part of Russia's military reserve, so this plane no doubt doubles as a troop transport. Word has it that we have stopped in Newfoundland because these planes are so fuel inefficient that they must island-hop their long-distance flights, so that they can keep drinking gasoline. Unless you ask one of the evangelists, who will tell you that we have stopped here to save an Eskimo or two.

As we enter the transit lounge, an Aeroflot representative hands each passenger a voucher printed in Russian for a complimentary Coke. I head toward the cafeteria, but stop short when I see the long line, each passenger with voucher in hand, anxious for the freebie. I see the heavyset evangelist trying to defend his place in line against the woman who had the facial towel. She is trying to squeeze in ahead of him, but he covers so much ground that there is not a chance of it.

"Now, just wait your turn, Maybell," he says, and she shrinks back behind him.

"I just thought I was here first, Emil."

I am discouraged by all of this and decide to take a seat and read. Before I have even cracked my book, there is someone standing over me holding out a pamphlet: "A Question You Must Answer."

I look up and notice Maybell, sans Coke. "Can I sit down?" she asks. "In case you have any questions about this literature."

"I was just going to get my free Coke," I offer, attempting to rise.

Maybell seats herself next to me and places her weathered hand on mine. "It's not worth it," she says. "Emil won't let anybody in ahead of him."

I have always wondered at people who drop the names of acquaintances I could not possibly know. Why did she think I would want to get ahead of Emil?

"Are you going to Russia?" she asks me with eyes wide open, as if she is already astonished at what my answer will be.

"Yes," I say.

Maybell bobs her head, full of understanding. She is about seventy, with faded blond hair gathered into bunches and rubber-banded like a harvest of dead grass. "Why?" she asks.

"I'm adopting a little boy."

"Praise the Lord!"

I smile. I like the approval my adoption plans tend to elicit.

"So, you feel the Lord working through you to bring this boy out of his misery and to America where he'll have a great deal to be grateful for."

Maybell says this as if it is some self-evident truth. "I don't think he's so miserable," I tell her. "He just needs a family."

Maybell will not go away empty-handed. "But you do think he'll have a better life in America," she says, nodding. This is no longer evangelism, it is conservative politics. Are there no liberal evangelists in the world?

I have thought a good deal about people's motivation for adoption. I have met prospective adoptive parents—mostly those who have never been abroad—who seem to feel that every foreign child yearns for a crack at life in America. But children who do not live in America can be happy, too. It is possible for a child to be happy in Guatemala, India, and Borneo. What Maybell has broached is the subject of ulterior motives: I want to be the father of a little boy, but what I really want is to get him to Kentucky Fried Chicken as soon as possible, don't I?

"I'm just trying to provide a healthy family life for him," I say, wondering why I am justifying the adoption to someone like Maybell.

She is not mollified. "Isn't that what I said?" she counters.

"No. You said I was bringing him to America because children who don't live in America are miserable."

Silence.

Maybell pushes a hand against one of her bundles of hair, looking away, collecting her thoughts. I sense her thinking that she has made some hideous mistake in sitting next to me and now she is looking for a mannerly exit. To my surprise, though, she comes back at me. Pointing at the pamphlet she has given me, she nods several times and then speaks. "Have you read it yet?"

I look down at the pamphlet again: "A Question You Must Answer." It is about salvation. "Not yet," I say.

Maybell strikes hard. "But you should," she admonishes me, smiling broadly and revealing every capped and filled tooth in her head. "You should. Because just like Christ, you, too, are providing salvation for someone. This little boy is waiting for you to save him."

Having said this, Maybell leans back in her seat and folds her hands in her lap, as if, at last, she has gotten what she wanted to say just right. Interestingly enough, I think about her words ... and then I reject them. I am not saving anybody. Pictures I have of Alyosha show him to be healthy, energetic, and with a sparkle of intelligence in his eyes—no bed sores, distended belly, or sunken cheeks. I had been told of adoptive parents who expected their children to have such features and then roundly rejected them when they discovered that the kids were generally in good health, physically and mentally, and had been well provided for in their orphanages. These parents had wanted to make a statement, but to do so they needed a physical and mental wreck of a child they could cosmetically redeem. In Maine this has happened more than once: the kids were not impoverished enough for their adoptive parents' needs. Within a year the children had to be removed from these families and placed elsewhere. I feel that my own needs simply compliment Alyosha's. He needs a family and I need a son. Is there more to it than that?

I turn to Maybell. "Thank you," I say. "Thank you for helping me clear something up in my head."

Maybell looks at me, smiling again. It is a smile of quiet satisfaction, the smile of a woman who savors cut flowers in crystal vases. Over the loudspeaker we are told to reboard our flight. I put out my hand and help Maybell up. Arm-in-arm we move along, down the corridor to the waiting plane. But we are overtaken by Emil, Coke in hand. "Maybell," he says. "It's not true. This isn't Greenland."

Maybell's expression falls. "It isn't? Then where are we, Praise the Lord?"

"New-Found-Land," he says, slowly, as if he doubts that such a place exists.

"Oh my," she says, palms to cheeks. "No Eskimos, then." As she says this she turns to me, smiling, making me feel as if I have saved the day for her.

Without another word we walk on, arm-in-arm toward Russia, I to embrace a little piece of it, Maybell to redeem the whole damn place.

We are descending again, precipitously. It is Shannon, Ireland, this time, although the evangelists believe that we are, at long last, landing in Russia.

At this point we have been underway for eight hours. It is 3:00 A.M. eastern time, which means 8:00 A.M. in Ireland. I already feel drawn out, rumpled, grimy. We disembark and are herded into the airport's transit lounge. It is bustling with activity, the concessions staffed by bright-eyed, rosy-cheeked Irish youths. In the distance a little boy is wailing on a penny whistle incompetently, with the effect being that of a soprano having her neck wrung while exclaiming "Ireland!"

I notice that all of the signs are bilingual—English and Gaelic. This strikes me as poignant, because so few in Ireland can speak or read Gaelic. The signs, therefore, amount to little more than a reminder that the language exists, on life support.

I head for the restroom, along with a dozen or so other men from the flight. When I enter I am struck by its pleasantness. It is the nicest public restroom I have ever seen, and big—a veritable concourse—with immaculate wash-up tables and shaving accessories dispensed by machine. I open the door to a stall and feel no compulsion to shout "Ai-ee!!" I am thoroughly satisfied.

While in Newfoundland I felt that I was somehow still connected to home, snuggled against North America the way the island is. But Ireland puts me cleanly on the "point-of-no-return" side of affairs. Once again we have been given chits for complimentary Cokes, and once again I find myself unwilling to compete with the likes of Emil to take advantage of it. I take a seat in the lounge and pull out the travel advisory for Russia the adoption agency had given me and that I have not yet had a chance to read.

"Ai-ee!!"

I am stunned by the admonishments of the document:

"If you are attacked on the streets, do not shout 'Police!' because the police have been known to join in the attacks. Instead, shout *'Pojhár!'* ('Fire!')."

"Do not leave any valuables in your hotel room, as the employees, including the management, have been known to ransack rooms in search of money and other goods."

"If someone looks at you on the street, gaze passively into the distance."

I suddenly find myself with a new and unwanted preoccupation. Having been told that travelers checks are useless in Russia and that even credit cards are largely unknown, I am carrying a large sum of cash, padding my body with it, hoping to remember where all the hiding places are (the left sock, the right-front jeans pocket, the chest pouch . . .). I am also acting as a "carrier" for Rainbow House, transporting several thousand dollars in a plain brown envelope, the money destined for the agency's contacts in Moscow. Last but not least, I have a bundle of "blatt"—small bribes (honey, hand lotion, shampoo) that I was told would be helpful in oiling the wheels of the Russian bureaucracy. "Blatt someone at every opportunity," I had read in a travel guide.

As I return to my travel advisory for more encouragement and affirmation, I am joined by Emil, who is holding his complimentary Coke in a fleshy hand. He sits down beside me but I do not take my eyes from the advisory. However, I know that he is looking at me. "Are you the one adopting a Russian kid?" he asks.

Maybell has obviously spread the word. I look up at Emil and force a smile, the sweetly ridiculous smile of the disinterested.

"Will you raise him a Christian?"

I have always felt most at ease with people who are direct, but the content of Emil's inquiry puts me off. "I haven't really thought about it," I say, gazing passively into the distance as the travel advisory recommends.

Emil starts to rummage in his shirt pockets, shifting the Coke from hand to hand.

"I already have the pamphlet," I say, preempting him.

Emil's eyebrows take flight. "Religion," he intones, "is the greatest gift you can give your child." Emil has the kind of voice that would carry cleanly through twelve inches of lead. His declaration is a clarion call to his fellow evangelists, several of whom hurriedly shuffle toward me. A minute later I am surrounded, gripped by the fear that they are going to touch me. I feel them closing in, the words "adoption," "Christian," "Russia" sussurrating about me like a swarm of flying insects. I imagine now that I am in competition with these people to get to my son first. I want to shout "Police!" No, "Fire!" (But what would the Irish think?) If I had my luggage I could blatt them away. Failing all of these devices, I stand, pick up my papers, and push my way through the evangelists, who part with great reluctance. Emil calls after me, but I do not respond. Instead, I enter the sanctuary of the restroom. Once again, I am alone with my thoughts.

Swept In

Chaos.

We have landed in Moscow. After fourteen hours of flight. The passengers are streaming from the plane like the Mississippi through a blown levee. I am being swept along, flotsamlike, between competing waves of sweating Russians and determined, militant evangelists. I see Maybell up ahead of me. I want to reach out to her, to say good-bye. But as I draw near she is consumed by the crowd like a drowning person. Emil continues to move ahead at the crest of the wave, because, as Maybell says, nobody gets ahead of Emil.

The crowd jams up at what ostensibly is passport control. There are ten booths but only two are open. It is like a cattle drive that has come to an abrupt halt at a narrow pass. This brings out the fight in even the passengers who were the most docile and abiding during the long flight. An elderly, stooped couple, draped with shoulder bags, shuffles toward a closed control booth, followed by a dozen or so others. Perhaps they are hoping to create critical mass there so an attendant will show up. But there is fat chance of it. The mob is being kept within bounds by a phalanx of milk-faced soldiers wearing the worried expressions of little boys who need to pee very badly. They race around frantically, waving their arms, leaping over barricades, shouting in Russian.

Is this the Red Army from which I was ducking and covering in Sister Helen Celene's first-grade class?

The crowd ignores the soldiers. It continues to probe and press, first here, then there, looking for openings, tender spots in their ranks. I have let my body go limp, content to be carried wherever the current takes me. Then, on the left flank, an opening. The Russians had placed two benches up against a glass sliding door leading to a closed booth. The elderly couple has managed to open the door and the man is prying the benches aside with his cane.

The old man and his wife push through the narrow opening they have created, and the entire herd is drawn in after them. First ten people are through, then twenty. The soldiers see this and four of them leap into the fray. They close the glass doors and replace the benches. Then, suddenly, they open up that booth and begin to examine the passports of those who got through.

Another booth opens, on the opposite side of the hall, and I am swept along to the right. Then that booth closes and I am swept to the left. The Russian passengers rise to the challenge and press their efforts ever onward, but the evangelists are steaming. It is hot as hell. I am then startled when I consider that perhaps this is what hell may be like.

Miraculously, after forty-five minutes of pandemonium, the booth directly in front of me opens up. Someone pushes me from behind and I find myself standing before a counter gazing up at the controller, who looks to be about fifteen. He takes my passport and visa and punches numbers into what looks like a 1930s vintage telephone switchboard. Then he stamps! stamps! stamps! my documents vengefully, the way I have seen it done in Germany. I take my papers and move on.

Contact

After the herd filters through the colander of control booths we recongeal into a narrow band of travelers, moving along through a tunnel formed by waiting friends and relatives on either side of us. I am supposed to be met by a liaison of Rainbow House, a woman named Nellie. There are hundreds and hundreds of faces, all searching, probing, the way mine is searching and probing. Then, ahead of me, a small, dark-haired woman with Asiatic features. She is holding a sign with my name on it.

It turns out that Nellie has been patiently waiting for hours for the delayed flight. She looks as if she had been on it herself. As I approach she puts out her hand and I reflexively dig the Rainbow House envelope out of my shirt and hand it to her. The money is accepted without a word.

After exchanging pleasantries, Nellie motions to me to follow her. A man in his thirties is standing beside her. He has the Pillsbury Doughboy face of Garth Brooks, but a cigarette hangs from his mouth in that distinctly Russian fashion, the butt seemingly glued to his lower lip, bobbing when he speaks. His name is Griescha. He salutes me, says "Okay!" in a manner suggesting that this is the only English word he knows. He follows me, along with Nellie, to the luggage carousel. There Griescha takes up my bags and the three of us march out into the open air of Moscow. Nellie and I get into Griescha's Russian-make compact. "Okay!" shouts Griescha, and we are off with a lurch and a screech. The car has no shock absorbers. It is like riding a roller skate.

Nellie is a Tatar, a descendant of those aggressive, hard-riding eastern tribes who harried the Russians for centuries. She speaks flawless English. I listen as Nellie fills my head with directives, procedures, and expectations. I hold onto the safety strap above my head as Griescha careers through the streets of Moscow, streets that have no painted lines and where the automobiles, not the pedestrians, have the right of way.

The sky begins to grow dark. A drop of rain strikes the windshield. Griescha jams on the brakes and I fly forward between the two front seats. I watch as Griescha pulls windshield wipers from under his seat, gets out, and affixes them to their stems. Then we are off again. I ask Nellie why he doesn't just keep the wipers in place. Her answer is concise: "Theft." I look out the window at the other cars, and by jingo, she is right — no wipers.

Griescha gets in and we roar off again. I settle back into my seat, try to remember where all of my cash is, and lean my head against the filmy window while taking in the sights of Moscow. I see gilded onion domes, shoulder-to-shoulder kiosks, soldiers and policemen, crumbling façades, curbside vodka vendors, and destitute-looking parks. The streets are swarming with people, but not a soul is smiling. Somewhere, in the distance, an accordionist is playing a lament.

I am in my son's country.

We have arrived at a formidable-looking apartment building somewhere in Moscow. Blocky and neglected, the building must have been something in its day. The street is fairly busy, with dour-faced Russians making their way in life. Maples, gnarled and unpruned, lean out into traffic. A raven perches on the hood of a Lada.

Nellie leans over the back of her seat and hands me a pen. "Write down your address so you won't get lost." Like a nine year old, I obediently comply. But the pen will not write. Griescha gives me his. I click it, and once again scratch nothingness across the paper. I reach into my pocket and retrieve a Bic. As Nellie spells and I write, I feel guilty that my American pen works and theirs does not.

We get out of the car and Griescha preempts me when I try to get at my bags. "Okay!" he says and takes them. I wonder whether his continued assistance calls for blatt.

Nellie tries the handle to the street door, but it seems frozen in place. She patiently works at the handle and tries again, but this time it spins freely. Finally, through some legerdemain, she opens the door. We enter a peelpaint vestibule. The marble steps are cracked and broken. The plaster walls look as if they have withstood a violent earthquake. I try to imagine what the place might have looked like eighty or ninety years earlier. I have a vision of ladies of fashion wafting through gas-lit halls to waiting *droshkies,* their arms interlocked with those of gentlemen in greatcoats who sport pointed beards in emulation of the czar. This image evaporates as an ancient, drunken man in house slippers emerges from behind a gaudily painted door and stumbles out onto the street.

Nellie and Griescha motion me to the elevator, but I hesitate. Neither the pen nor the door handle worked. Why on earth would I want to risk life and limb on the elevator? We wait for the machine to descend. Then the door opens. It has stopped about a foot above the floor. Griescha hauls my bags onto it as if he is loading a pickup. Nellie and I climb into a car as narrow as a coffin, and we are off.

We exit on the fifth floor. The corridor is dark and vacant. Nellie knocks at apartment 5A. There is a pattering of feet beyond the door. Then a serial turning of locks, one after the other, until three cylinders have spun. The door opens and a woman of about thirty-five greets us. She is fair of complexion, her hair tied back behind her head, her features careworn, but brightened by a smile. She bows in the self-effacing way of someone who knows no English and feels this to be a disadvantage. But then she surprises me. "Welcome to my home," she says, softly, punctuating this with another bow.

Her name is Lena. She takes me to my room. It is spacious and bookladen, with an upright piano against one wall. A balcony opens over a courtyard. Ravens perch on the balcony railing. They stare up at me, seeming somehow expectant. "Do you like?" asks Lena as she throws open the balcony doors, shooing the ravens in the process.

"It's beautiful," I answer. "I hope I'm not putting you out."

Lena looks at me. "Oh yes, indeed," she says, smiling, not quite comprehending.

Nellie and Griescha hover on the threshold, waiting patiently as Lena primps the room. When she is finished they enter. "I hope you are happy," says Lena, hesitantly, unsure of her English. Then she is gone.

Nellie tells me to sit tight for three days. "On the fourth day we will go to see your son," she says. "You should try to see some of the city in the meantime." Then she asks for $150 in cash. This will cover the costs of having Griescha act as my driver for the trips to the orphanage, the U.S. embassy, etcetera. As I peel the money from its roll, Griescha's expression brightens and he licks his lips. Then the two of them pass into the dark corridor and disappear from the apartment.

After Nellie and Griescha leave, I go out into the tiny kitchen. Lena is sitting at the table, absently stirring a cup of tea while she stares out the window. When she sees me she jumps up and begins to wait on me—tea and cakes. I repeatedly thank her with one of the fragments of Russian I packed in my head before departure. *"Spaseeba!"*

Lena sits down and joins me. She immediately begins to tell me about her life in Russia. She is a theater critic and her husband, Igor, is an actor (what a combination!). They have two children, Katya and Sasha. She tells me how difficult life is, how uncertain her days are. Then, plaintively, "I hate my life, but I love my country."

I try to respond to her but am unprepared for this intensity of engagement. "Your children must give you great pleasure," I say.

Lena looks at me and smiles. "Then put sugar in it. We have a lot of sugar." I am not sure if I am speaking too fast or using too complex a vocabulary.

Lena tells me that she feels Russians and Americans have much in common. "We both have the passion," she says.

The passion. Perhaps the Russians on the street are not particularly unhappy; perhaps they are unsmiling because they are brooding on matters of great philosophical importance. In modern memory, they have known a revolution, two world wars fought on their soil, a terror famine, Stalinist rule, and now, the loss of their country. Americans have experienced none of this. It makes me think of the movie *Dr. Zhivago.* I recall the scene of the Russian people swarming to the dead poet's grave and Alec Guinness's striking line: "No one loves poetry like a Russian." I compare this to the frivolousness of so much of modern American poetry, recited with bells and whistles to garner the interest of the tiny audience. But Russian poetry bears the collective memory of their darkest—and most passionate—days. For this reason it is taken seriously.

I look up at Lena. "I think we have passion for different things."

Lena raises her eyebrows. "Yes?"

"You protect and cherish your past, but Americans are in love with innovation, the future, and therefore know very little about their past." I stop myself short, sensing that I have said too much, that I have really stumped Lena this time.

"Robert," she says, calling me by my name for the first time. "Just don't let our children forget where they came from."

I realize who she means by "our children." She is speaking about the Russian children being adopted by Americans. "Lena, I will never let my son forget that his blood is Russian."

Lena smiles and nods. She gets up to heat more tea. I watch as she fumbles with the stove. The phone rings. She crosses the floor, picks up the receiver and says "Hello." Then she shouts "HELLO!" Finally, she hangs up the phone, sighing with resignation, because, like many other things in this troubled country, it too is broken.

Saturday, July 3, 1993

It is late evening. I have slept for a few hours and feel on top of things again. The apartment is dead silent. I sit up in bed and look toward the balcony doors. Although it is 9:00 P.M., the sun is still shining brightly, reflecting off the goldleaf of the onion dome of a local church. I rise, walk over to the doors, open them, and step out onto the balcony. Then, recalling the door handle and the pen, I quickly step back. It is enough to gaze out over the neighborhood from the recesses of the apartment itself.

Below me all is calm. An old woman, rocking on bowed legs, pulls her shopping cart along; three schoolgirls with arms interlocked skip and giggle; a mother tows her son — perhaps seven years old — by the arm as he wails his resistance.

I thought Russian children were less complicated to raise?

I step out into the vestibule, where Lena and her husband Igor have installed an elaborate jungle gym. With swinging bars, climbing ladder, and ropes, they have made excellent use of limited space to give their children an indoor source of physical recreation.

The kitchen door is closed. I hesitate for a moment and then gently prod it open. There is a man sitting at the table. He is about thirty-two, of medium stature, bearded, and with dark, wavy hair. He gazes up at me. The look in his eyes says, "I can't believe I'm in Moscow."

Ah, another American.

His name is Barry and he is here to adopt a nineteen-month-old girl. He lives with his wife and children in Florida. This is not their first time at it: a couple of years ago they adopted a little boy from Romania. They are having so much fun that they thought they would do it again.

We compare notes. "Did you have to give Nellie one hundred fifty dollars as soon as you got here?"

"Yes."

"Isn't Griescha something? Do you think he's a wheeler-dealer?"

"Yes."

"Did you see how they keep their windshield wipers under their seats?"

"Yes!"

I tell Barry that I will feel free and easy only when I am airborne with my son. "What's your biggest worry?" I ask him. His answer is immediate: "That I will lose weight." I take this as a reference to either the unavailability of food or to its quality.

I show Barry my room. "It's big," he says. "What are those things on the balcony?"

"Ravens. I asked for a room with ravens. Didn't you?"

Barry does not know how to take this. Then his eyes brighten and he laughs. I know immediately that we will get along. Barry reciprocates and shows me his room. It, too, is spacious. We soon learn that Lena and Igor have wedged themselves into the smallest room in the apartment so that we could have the two biggest bedrooms.

We return to the kitchen, where Lena is now at work. She is steeping tea, frying eggs, and slicing meats. With a few swift moves of her hands she has set a table with seven or eight offerings, a culinary quilt of Russia. As Barry and I dig in, she takes a place at the edge of the table. Her face is drawn and tired looking, but her features revive somewhat as she watches us eat. Barry feels compelled to speak. "This is a nice apartment," he says.

Lena nods and smiles. "I hope you like."

"Where are your children?" I ask.

"They are in the country, with relatives. I will go see them in a few days."

The conversation is going well. Perhaps it was the initial excitement that had compromised her comprehension earlier. "You must be looking forward to it," says Barry.

Lena inclines her ear, then her expression brightens. "Thank you!"

The talk turns to money. At the moment the U.S. dollar is worth about a thousand rubles. Lena explains to us that, whenever possible, we should try to buy things with rubles. "Because," she says, "it will be better."

What she means is "cheaper."

Lena informs us, for example, that she has obtained tickets for us for the evening's performance of "The Nutcracker." "Tickets twenty dollars," she says gravely, nodding her head.

Barry and I immediately offer to reimburse her. Lena waves us off. "Is okay," she says. "I pay with rubles. Ticket was only six hundred rubles." About sixty cents.

Barry is bolder than I am. He asks Lena about her salary. I turn away, embarrassed. But in the way of someone living in a country whose difficulties are off the scale and therefore obvious to the world, Lena has no qualms about answering the question. "I earn thirty-five dollars a month," she says.

Barry and I look at each other. "And my husband," she volunteers, "earns thirty." Before we can react she has turned the tables on us. "And what about you?" she asks.

Lena's question puts me on the spot because I do not want to make her feel bad in any way. "More than thirty dollars," I say before burying my face in my tea.

"How much more?" she asks.

Barry looks at me as if to say "Well, go on and tell her."

I tell her that I make over $2000 a month. "But that's before taxes," I quickly add. "And, to tell you the truth, that's not considered a great deal of money in America."

Lena nods as if she already knows that. Then she tells us that her rent is five cents a month. Her eyes seem to say, see, it all comes out in the wash.

Money is constantly on my mind these days. I am almost obsessed with it. Not with the attainment of more, but with the utilitarian use of what I have. After having given Nellie the $150, I am left with $1000 in cash; $450 of that will go to Lena and Igor for room and board at the rate of $30 per day. Although reasonable by American standards, I recognize, intellectually, that I am giving them one of their monthly salaries every day of my stay. Yet I am happy to do this. I find Lena so generous and sweet that I am honored to be able to make life a bit easier for her and her family.

Beyond the room and board, I have been told to set aside $200 for Alyosha's U.S. visa. I am still seething about this. It is a ridiculous fee. I am adopting a child who will be no burden to society, and yet my own government is charging me as much to admit him to residency as I have paid for his air ticket home. I am aware that the words "political asylum" at any U.S. port of entry would obviate the need for a visa on the spot, but such thoughts get me nowhere.

I go on with my calculations. Alyosha will also need a physical before he gets his visa. Nellie has told me that it can be done either at the American clinic for $120 or with the Russians for $70. Guess where I am taking him. Once again it is my own government that, like Emil, has muscled itself to the head of the line for its share of the take.

That will leave me with $280 in pocket money, so I must be careful.

The phone rings. Lena picks it up. It is Griescha. He wants to take Barry and me around Moscow—for $3 an hour. The price is good, of course, but I do not want to get into the habit of peeling off money right away. Neither does Barry. We therefore decline, but tell him that we might be interested later.

Diplomacy is everything.

We have made a serious dent in the tomatoes, eggs, cucumbers, bread, and silver dollar–size pancakes, of which there was a veritable mountain. Whenever Barry and I slow in our eating, Lena wrings her hands. "You don't like?" she frets. "Oh, no," says Barry. "It's very good." As he says this he rolls his hands over his protruding belly. He looks up at me and I can immediately tell that his concern about losing weight has been allayed.

Sleep beckons again. As we rise from the table I thank Lena for the food. "It was delicious," I say. She looks at me. "Yes, of course we will have fishes if you like," she answers. Then she stares at me. "You understand when I speak English?"

"Of course."

Lena beams.

Diplomacy is everything.

— Sunday, July 4, 1993 —

I slept well, but briefly, waking up at about 3:30 A.M. when the sun came streaming through my window. This is the north.

We were supposed to go to the U.S. embassy tomorrow, to get an appointment for a visa interview. But Nellie called this morning—the embassy will be closed in celebration of the Fourth of July. Despite their remove from the land of E. Pluribus Unum, our foreign service bureaucrats want their perks, too, on the national holiday.

Barry and I sit in the kitchen, opposite one another at the small table. Lena is working furiously at the stove to prepare our breakfast. I have always been uncomfortable having someone I know wait on me with anything resembling servility. But here I accept this without protest, both because hospitality runs hot in the Russian blood and because this is, after all, a business arrangement in which board is part of the package. Yet I still find myself wishing that Lena were a severe, instructive matron with a tightly coiled bun rather than the gentle, long-suffering Slav. It would be easy to tell such a person that the tea is cold rather than having to wait for Lena to leave the kitchen before surreptitiously sneaking to the kettle for a warm-up, so as not to hurt her feelings.

Under normal conditions I would be thrilled to be where I am: Russia, Moscow. But I am restless, unable to relish the culture, because both today and tomorrow there will be absolutely no activity on the adoption front. My plane ticket, bargain basement item that it is, requires me to leave Russia on July 18 or else pay hundreds of dollars, at least, to have the tickets changed. Barry, on the other hand, has purchased an open ticket, at top dollar, so his burden of preoccupation is that much lighter than mine. We exchange thoughts on the seemingly eternal wait for something concrete to happen. Our every comment is punctuated by Lena's bending over the table to slip in another platter of bread or sliced cheese or *piroshki,* for which we offer our *Spaseeba*s.

After breakfast, Barry and I decide to take a walk to the Kremlin. With cameras in hand we head for the door. Lena calls after us. She hands us three keys, one for each lock to the apartment. "But downstairs you must push the numbers," she says, referring to the entrance panel studded with black plastic buttons. "Sixty-seven."

"Spaseeba!"

Barry and I hurry down the ten flights of stairs, neither of us wanting to risk a go at the elevator. We exit the building, stepping out under overcast skies onto Potapovsky Prospect. The façades of some of the buildings on this residential street are beautiful, reminiscent of old Europe; but they, like the street itself, have not been maintained for decades. Whole cornices, pulling away from façades, are held in place by jury-rigged slats of wood or metal rods. Whole slabs of sidewalk are thrown heavenward by the roots of immense sycamores. In other places the sidewalk is entirely absent—perhaps trampled into dust by the heavy pedestrian traffic. I like this neighborhood. It looks as if it is being reclaimed by nature and I am, therefore, part of a process. I hope it is not the only process I will be part of during my stay in Russia.

I ask Barry if he knows where the Kremlin is. He tells me that he can see a big building with a red star from his bedroom window. So we head off in that direction until, turning a corner, the building and its star rise up before us in the distance. Like the wise men (minus one) we continue to follow that star. We become part of a crowd, pushing and maneuvering and shoving ourselves along just like the Russians. No one pays us any attention, not even a glance, even though our Americanness is obvious. It is in our "happy to be here" walk, in our held-at-the-ready cameras, and especially in our smiles and laughter.

I find my eyes being drawn to every little Russian boy I see, looking for visible differences between them and American kids. Physically, they all seem to have straight hair and there is a preponderance of those lovely, wide-set Russian eyes. Some of them have the look of the imp about them, but they appear far less antic than American boys. Then a woman's voice cries out "Alyosha!"

I stop and turn, searching, searching the street. A beautiful young Russian woman is calling after her little boy, who has lagged behind to stare at a pile of Snickers bars being hawked from a card table. "Alyosha!" she hollers, and my heart surges. He, too, is beautiful, with straight blond hair awash over his brown eyes. I watch as he pulls himself away from the chocolate and runs to catch up with his mother.

I ask Barry if he finds himself staring at every little Russian girl he sees.

"All the time."

The star is straight ahead of us. We cross a broad boulevard and then traverse an overpass. Ever since we left the apartment the skies have been growing darker. Now the clouds are beginning to boil. But still we press on with deliberation, as if under that red star our two children will be lying in swaddling clothes, their arms outstretched to us, the seraphim singing on high.

"This walk is not distracting me enough," I confide to Barry.

"I know what you mean. I had expected to get here and basically have the kids waiting for us. But everything still seems so uncertain."

"We'll see them in three days," I tell him. "But it seems like such a long time to wait." Once again I realize, in a powerful way, that commiseration is very real comfort. It is good to be in Moscow with another American who is going through the same experience and with whom I can think out loud. Even complaining is therapeutic, if only because it is a way of showing that we can take it.

Suddenly we are standing across the street from the building with the red star on it. The problem is that it is not the Kremlin. I don't know why I didn't recognize this earlier. "Our minds are elsewhere," says Barry, adding, "I just wish something would happen soon."

His wish is granted. The heavens are rent asunder and the rain pours down upon us in buckets. We run for cover, tucking ourselves into a very shallow doorway, so that our heads stay dry but the toes of our shoes are drenched, soaking up water like a wick. We watch as traffic comes to a standstill and the drivers hop out to install their windshield wipers.

After ten minutes the rain relents to a drizzle, so we head home, sans Kremlin. By the time we arrive on Potapovsky Prospect the rain has ceased and the clouds are beginning to break up. The street has been washed, the worn and ruptured façades glisten in the emerging sunlight, freshets stream from broken gutters and splatter on the sidewalks. The branches of the sycamores are heavy with water, and *babushkas* throw windows open to admit the purified air. Everything smells new, anything is possible again: finding the Kremlin, adopting a child.

Barry and I push "67" on the entrance panel and wait for the electric latch to open. Then we wait some more.

Well, almost anything is possible.

Neither Barry nor I have ever been to the ballet. For some reason I am slightly ashamed of this. Perhaps because I am in Russia, where culture is written with a capital C.

"The Nutcracker" is being performed by the Kremlin Ballet. The theater is inside the Kremlin wall. This time we find the Kremlin with no problem at all—because Lena takes us there by the hand. Along the way we must cross a broad avenue. We use a pedestrian underpass that is lined with kiosks and impromptu businesses set up on card tables. Vendors are selling cigarettes, books, flowers, and sundries. The ubiquitous vodka stand is there as well, selling vodka by the shot. I have noticed that these stands are always tended by either a teenager or an old woman.

When we emerge we are bearing down on the Kremlin itself. As we draw closer, it becomes obvious that this is the only part of Moscow whose physical appearance is maintained with anything resembling attention. St. Basil's Cathedral looks exactly as I had expected it to: party-colored and incongruously placed next to the federal-looking Kremlin itself, like a wedding cake set next to a cinder block.

To get to the theater we must pass over a cobbled bridge . . . along with half of Moscow. I am in awe of the number of men, women, and young children swarming toward the theater. They are dressed up for it, not elaborately, but no doubt in the best clothes they have. Barry and I look like street bums in our jeans and T-shirts.

Lena struggles with us toward the front entrance, where we become firmly lodged in the bottleneck of humanity. Then she signals us to move sideways. We follow her lead, extricate ourselves from the crowd, and enter the building through another door. "This is for the critics," she says.

The theater is very attractive from an architectural point of view. It is a modern structure, heavily invested with glass and marble, extensively carpeted in red. We walk inside with our sixty-cent tickets and get seats near the stage. The theater fills up quickly until both the lower level and the balcony are packed. Despite my lack of interest in ballet, the realization that I am about to see and hear Tchaikovsky in Moscow fills me with anticipation.

The hour strikes for the performance, but I do not see any orchestra. Then, from two large 1950s-vintage speakers on either side of the stage, the overture to the suite begins to crackle and rasp.

The orchestra is seated.

I realize immediately that we are not going to see a first-class company. My eyes continue to focus on the speakers, which are blaring so harshly that they bulge with every crescendo. As the overture subsides the first dancers spring onto the stage, and then more appear. Every footfall is like a hammer blow. I look about at the Russian audience and every face is rapt. They are captivated by the spectacle. Next to me a mother and her young son are holding hands. The boy is on the edge of his seat, his face filled with an expectancy that Americans reserve for thrillers or westerns. I look back to the stage, at the wild amalgam of performers who are dancing their hearts out. It is colorful: the costumes are first class and beautifully designed, the sets wildly surrealistic. The performers and the Russian audience are all but reaching out to one another. It is obvious that they are in love. I begin to feel guilty for allowing the least critical thought to enter my head, regardless through which door I entered the theater.

All of a sudden someone in the balcony begins to shout. I turn around and look up to see a tall, bearded, disheveled man standing at the rail, making a speech in a booming baritone, his arm athrust in the manner of Lenin. Now he is in competition with the dancers on the stage, who seem to have picked up the tempo in an effort to retain the public's attention. The man seems mad or possessed, not drunk. He finally finishes his speech and the audience applauds him. I notice that, while their applause for the stage troupe has been generous, that for the man in the balcony is more spontaneous and heartfelt.

"The Dance of the Sugarplum Fairies," the only part of "The Nutcracker" that I can immediately identify, is disappointing. It is more like the "March of the Wooden Soldiers" or "Breakers at Big Sur." Still, the Russians drink, drink, drink of this spectacle. This is culture, albeit a bad rendering of culture. But the Russians' passion for it endows it with a respectability worth being crushed alive for. This is ballet for the masses. As such, it is affordable and valiantly flamboyant. I think of the times back in Maine when we have had first-rate performances from New York go poorly attended in our arts centers because Vanna White's pregnancy had captured the imagination of a TV nation. Here the lame shufflings of ballet's third stringers have packed the house to the rafters.

After the performance Barry and I spill out into the lobby with the crowd. Barry goes over to a souvenir counter while I speak with Lena. She is standing with a couple in their thirties, clearly Americans. Lena introduces them to me as Babs and Rick. They are from Duluth and are also here to adopt. Babs seizes my hand and pumps it wildly. "I can conceive," she confides to me, "I just can't hold them."

I am thunderstruck by this revelation. All I can say is, "My name is Bob."

I look over at her husband. With his ring of windblown blond hair and slightly stooped posture, he seems to have been separated from Art Garfunkel at birth. Rick says nothing to me. I reach over and take his hand, which is like lifting a pump handle.

Babs is loquacious, horsey, and animated. She is certainly friendly and interested in meeting me, but she reveals all. In the next five minutes she tells me about her three miscarriages, including the dates of their occurrences. She and Rick are in Russia to adopt a five-year-old boy and an infant girl. I look back at Rick, who is pivoting slowly back and forth on his heels, looking bored. No conversation there. Babs asks about my son. "He's seven," I tell her, and before I can utter another syllable she shouts, "Isn't that wonderful!"

It *is* wonderful, but there is so much more. However, I cannot get a word in edgewise and decide to bail out. I excuse myself and mosey over to the gift counter, passing Barry, who is headed back toward Lena and the Duluths. For a moment I consider warning him, but he is old enough to fend for himself.

When things finally break up I join Barry in front of the theater. Lena and the Duluths have gone on. "Did you meet Babs?" I ask Barry.

His response is immediate. "I can conceive but I can't hold them?"

"That's it."

We set off together for home. We arrive at the apartment building on Potapovsky Prospect, push "67," and wait for nothing. Eventually another tenant comes along, pushes his number, and we follow him through the door.

Lena is not home yet, but we meet Igor for the first time. Dark, his head awash in black hair, his features robust yet careworn, he greets us in bathrobe and slippers. We have woken him up. "We're sorry," I apologize, "for getting you out of bed."

Igor waves us off and shuffles through the apartment to the kitchen table, inviting us to sit with him. "Don't worry about it," he says affably, his English good but halting. "Have some tea."

As he pours I notice that he is constantly rubbing his abdomen. "Are you all right?" I ask.

"Yes, yes," he says. "I always have this problem."

"Maybe you should see a doctor."

"I have medicine," he says. Barry and I watch as Igor takes out a bottle of vodka, fills a soda glass to brimming, and begins to down it, pausing only once to say "*Na zdorovye.*"

We sit up a while longer, sipping tea and getting acquainted with our host. Igor is a chain-smoker, but whenever he lights up he graciously excuses himself from the kitchen. When he returns he picks up exactly where he left off. He is telling us of all there is to see in Moscow, naming streets and subway stops with casual abandon, as if Barry and I will have no trouble remembering these exotic place names. Igor must sense this, for he smiles and nods. "I am sorry," he says. "You have not so much time here and I am telling you things you cannot possibly remember."

As with Lena, Barry and I are charmed by Igor, who has captivated us with his openness and sincerity, beneath which pulses yet another brooding Russian heart.

Monday, July 5, 1993

I was able to sleep a little later today—until 4:40 A.M.. I was awakened not so much by the early sun as by the squawking of the ravens. These birds actually chatter with one another at close range, as if holding a conversation. When I throw open the balcony doors in the morning they disperse. They seem to do so not so much out of fear as disgust with me for disturbing their salon.

When I enter the kitchen I greet Lena, who is hard at work at the stove. Barry is already at the table sipping his coffee and watching CNN, looking as if he never left southern Florida, wanting only a flowered shirt. I take my place opposite him and Lena quickly sets a cup of tea in front of me before flying back to the stove to fetch my breakfast.

The phone rings. Lena picks it up. Then she holds the receiver out to us. "An American?" she says, doubtfully.

My heart quickens. If this is a call from home perhaps it is an emergency. Why else would someone from the States call Russia? I look at Barry and push the receiver at him, my expression imploring him to take the phone, as if his doing so will make it his emergency and not mine.

Barry defers to me. I press the receiver to my ear and am rewarded with a harsh crackle of static. Suddenly, out of the heart of this sonic mist, a voice emerges. My God, it's Babs.

I mouth her name to Barry and he chokes on his coffee. I listen through the fuzz as Babs begins her narrative. Something about the Bolshoi, tonight, tickets, gift. It is like having a telegram read to me over the phone with only key words coming through the continuing disturbance. Then I consider that this is a blessing, sparing me the agony of listening to the whole story.

I try to reply to Babs, but she shouts, "Speak up!" So I shout into the receiver, but she still cannot make me out. I cup my hand over the mouthpiece and shout again. There is a roar of static in reply. This is a horrible, horrible experience. It is like having a hole drilled into my head. Finally, there is a strange interlude of relative silence. Taking advantage of the calm, Babs speaks her piece again.

After we hang up I sit back down, shaking my head. Barry looks at me and says, "Well?"

I tell him that Babs and Rick are going to the Bolshoi this evening.

"So?"

"So she wanted to know if we have tickets too."

Barry shrugs. "Where did they get theirs?"

"Babs said they were a gift from the Russian people."

"What?"

"She says they were a gift. . . ."

"A gift?"

"From the Russian people."

"Why?"

"For taking their children." That is what Babs had said: She and her husband had been given the tickets as a gift from the Russian people for taking their children.

Barry looks at me as if I am losing my mind. "But why would someone give them tickets to the Bolshoi?" he asks, half rhetorically.

I throw him a look that questions his lack of understanding. "They're a gift!" I chide.

Barry hoists his coffee cup in salute. "From the Russian people!"

It sounds so odd to me. It is my understanding that most Russians are, at root, anti-adoption. They view the export of their children, with some justification, as the bleeding off of their culture. I have read similar things about Polish adoptions, which is perhaps why they are so difficult. Yet my willingness to understand this view is tempered by another aspect of the Russian attitude toward adoption: children in Russian orphanages must first be offered to Russian families. Only if no Russian shows interest in a child can he or she be offered for foreign adoption. However, Russians will not adopt any child who has the least defect. A lazy eye, a missing digit, a speech impediment—things that would be unlikely to impede an adoption in the United

States — are considered grounds for rejection here, and the child is labeled unadoptable.

Barry is also privy to this information. Both of us have been wondering what the nature of our own children's "defects" will be. The pictures we have show them to be healthy and, as far as we can tell, happy. They are beautiful children. Why would a Russian family not want one of these kids? In two days we may have our answer.

After breakfast Barry and I decide to go to the Kremlin, now that we know where it is. The day is mild, overcast, and breezy. We head down Potapovsky Prospect, through the underpass. Twenty minutes later we are standing in Red Square. Lena has given us a sheaf of tickets to the various exhibits and museums. They are entirely in Russian, so it is hard to say what is what. We soon discover, however, that the tickets work in a capricious manner. We enter a small church *cum* museum. A squat, kerchiefed babushka shaped like a nesting doll is sitting on a wooden chair. She tears off a fistful of tickets with her thick hands and waves us in. There is not much to see: a few paintings, some relics in glass cases, and a few frescoes. We exit the church and head for the next one. Another *matrioshka*-shaped babushka on another chair, only this one shows contempt for the tickets I hold out to her and reviles us in Russian, driving us back out into the street.

The next museum — the Kremlin grounds are studded with them — we treat with cautious abandon. There is yet another hardened babushka inside the door. When she sees us she smiles invitingly, her narrow eyes becoming almond slivers floating on cherry-red cheeks. Barry and I enter, but when I extend the tickets she frowns. Then she tosses a couple of quick glances about herself, looks back at us, and feathers her palm. Ah, she wants blatt. I steal a glance past her into the vestibule of the museum. There is nothing extraordinary there. No, I will not blatt this woman.

Barry and I mosey over to Lenin's tomb, but it is closed today. We will have to come back tomorrow. Rumor has it that Lenin will be removed and buried soon. Time is of the essence if I wish to see the discredited founder of a defunct empire before he is dropped into a hole and covered with dirt.

Back out in Red Square we are approached by a young, blond Russian who is about twenty years old. He introduces himself as Victor and asks if we would like a tour of the Red Square attractions. His manner is earnest and sweet. He is what one would call in the States a go-getter, trying his wings as a fledgling capitalist in the new and open business climate of his country.

"How much?" Barry asks.

Victor holds up all the fingers of his right hand. "Five," he says.

Without batting an eye and wearing his best poker face, Barry shoots back "Four."

Victor smiles. "Ah," he says, "there is no doubt that you are Americans. Okay," he says affably, "four."

Victor, like most Russians I have met, is superbly versed in his country's history. Dates, people, and events spill from his lips like the various facets of a favorite epic tale. The combination of his cultural awareness and his friendly, self-effacing personality draws me in. I realize that Barry and I have a real find on our hands. As Victor takes us through St. Basil's, the crown jewel of Red Square, I am also filled with a strange pathos, born of the realization that people like him, although still common in Russia, may soon be a dying breed now that we Americans have landed with our insidious popular culture. I think of my own students, who are blissfully ignorant of books and untethered to any meaningful acquaintance with history, culture, or language, their attention being fully consumed by videos, sitcoms, and MTV. There was a time in America when school was the only show in town. Now teaching has become a matter of selling the unwanted to the nonbuying. Americans, sad to say, are widely regarded as superficial. Our historical culture has been supplanted by the untransmissible, fleeting popular culture of misleading images and subliminal messages to buy, buy, buy. If I could have just one Victor in my class each semester, teaching would be sublime.

After our tour, Victor asks Barry and me what we are doing in Russia. When he learns of our adoption plans he nods approvingly. "That's very good," he says. "That you are willing to take care of these children." Then he spots a trio of young, disoriented-looking Americans in the distance. Victor's eyes blaze. He hears opportunity knocking again. "I think I must go," he says. We shake hands and bid our farewells. I am left wondering what Victor will be like in five years. I harbor a fragile hope that the Russian cultural intensity is genetic and that my son will have inherited this quality as well.

"He was a pretty nice guy," says Barry. "And I learned a lot."

"He was a gift," I add, "from the Russian people."

Tuesday, July 6, 1993

Once again Barry and I conduct our breakfast ritual, he sitting on the window side of the little table watching CNN news, I planted opposite him by the phone with my hands wrapped around a teacup, and Lena shuffling about the kitchen, waiting on us, alternately serving up eggs and lamenting her life. I feel as if I have been living here for years.

Nellie calls. It is embassy day. Her voice carries a sense of urgency. "We must get there early," she says, "and we must get an appointment for a visa interview within the time frame of your stay in Russia."

"Of course," I agree, not knowing exactly what it is that I am agreeing to. "But what do you mean by 'interview'?"

Nellie explains that in order for a Russian child's visa to be granted, all of his adoption paperwork must be in absolutely flawless order: original birth certificate, amended birth certificate listing me as the father, orphanage release form, judicial papers stating that the child is free and clear for adoption. "And I must translate all of these papers," she adds, "for you and Barry and Babs and Rick." She goes on to explain that an embassy official will interview me to verify that I understand what all of the documents contain.

"So I'll have to do my homework," I concede.

"Right."

After hanging up I pass this information to Barry, who looks relieved that things are beginning to happen. I tell him that Nellie will meet us outside the building at 8:30 A.M. and we will take the metro—the famous Moscow Metro—with her to the embassy.

At the appointed hour, Nellie is standing outside the front door. We follow her at a brisk pace down Potapovsky Prospect toward the metro station. It is a busy business day: the stores are crammed with customers, makeshift stands stacked with Snickers bars line the curbs. We descend into the bowels of the metro via the longest and most crowded escalator I have ever seen—if it collapsed it would take half of Moscow with it.

This metro is as clean and pleasant as I had been told. The whole thing seems built of polished marble. At this particular station I see none of the art pieces that are supposed to line its corridors. Perhaps they have been removed because of the titanic surge in Moscow's crime rate since the Communist government fell. Nellie steps up to a window and purchases our tokens: plastic tiddly-wink chips. The fare is about two cents.

The train rolls in, bright and clean and graffiti-free. Within the next minute we are swooshing down the line toward the embassy station. There is no conversation on the train. All the faces are dour and disconnected from anything resembling life. These are Moscow's New Yorkers.

We emerge somewhere between McDonald's and the U.S. embassy. As we approach the embassy the pedestrian traffic thickens considerably. It is sheathed in scaffolding, so that a coherent view of the whole structure is impossible. Outside there is a Russian police officer or army officer—I cannot tell which—sorting those who head for the embassy door. Most are sent to the right, to stand in line along an extensive plywood wall. These are Russians, mostly dark men with the aspect of Gypsies, huddling and smoking and waiting to conduct their business within. Barry and I, on the other hand, barely wink our American passports and the guard defers to us, waving us through the doors, with Nellie stealing along in our wake like a thief in the night.

We are directed to a waiting room by a Marine guard. The room has the feel of a welfare clinic: a row of chairs against a wall facing a long, bare counter with scratched plexiglas windows. A phalanx of other Americans has already gathered there—more hopeful adoptive parents. They make efforts to become acquainted with one another, as people sharing a common lot tend to do. Nellie leans over to me and tells me that some of these people (the ones with absolutely no paperwork in their hands) are here ad hoc, taking their chances on a child by drifting from orphanage to orphanage. It seems fantastic that they harbor the slightest hope of succeeding. Yet these people seem to be the only ones smiling, as if they know something the rest of us do not. Or perhaps ignorance is simply bliss.

Nellie relates a story to me of an American woman from California (where else?) who runs a Russian adoption racket. "She promises groups of Americans Russian children, collects thousands of dollars from them, brings them to Russia, and gives them maps showing the locations of the orphanages."

"That's it?"

"Then they're on their own," she adds.

"Is her name Marilyn?"

Nellie looks at me. "I don't think so."

Within twenty minutes some eighteen Americans have gathered. This must represent a quorum, for an embassy official finally appears, entering through a door I had not even noticed. She is a small woman in her thirties, with short, dark hair. She rolls her hands continuously, like a housefly. Her steps are light and rapid, in the manner of Anna Karenina, and her entrance is enough to cast us into silence. She looks at each of our faces in turn. It is as if she is challenging us to speak unbidden. I regard her hard chin and small, tight mouth, and then it dawns on me: I know this look and posture. My God, this woman was once a nun.

Her name is Anne Reese, but she could just as easily be Sister Jude Therese, the scourge of sixth grade at Sacred Heart Grammar School in Jersey City.

She speaks in a terse, clipped manner. "You will need the following forms in the following format. If any are missing or not properly signed, or unaccompanied by a translation, the interview will be terminated." Then she proceeds to list the forms. Nellie leans over to me. "I've never seen this woman before," she says.

"Is she far worse than the Witch of the East?" I ask.

The group of Americans seems intimidated by the official's stern demeanor. We listen as Anne relates an anecdote about a family that had flown to Moscow from Vladivostok and came to the embassy lacking one signature. They had to fly back to Vladivostok to get this signature. Even I am horrified by this image. Vladivostok is on the other side of Russia, near Japan. Nellie senses my consternation. "Don't worry," she says, "domestic air travel in Russia is cheap."

Anne's speech lasts ten minutes, and she solicits no questions. When she is finished she directs us to a window where we can make appointments for our visa interview—if we dare. As she turns to go back through her door, a young American couple is just arriving. They ask Anne to tell them what she has already told the rest of us. "Of course," she says, "one week from today at the same time." And then she is gone.

Nellie looks at me and smiles. "Don't worry," she says, "it's not as bad as she makes it seem. Your papers will be in order."

"I'm not afraid of her," I reply lamely, like a juvenile. Then Barry and I sign up for an interview. Mine will be on Friday, July 16 at 1:30 P.M.. Ten days away, it seems like an eternity.

Back outside, Nellie releases us from her care. "Tomorrow we go to see the children," she says. My blood rushes. I fall completely out of touch with my feelings. I am not nervous or fearful or tense or anything that I can put my finger on. This is the way with the unreal: The only words we have at our disposal to describe it are rooted in reality, and they just will not do.

Barry and I decide to go to Lenin's tomb. It is also in Red Square, between the mammoth GŪM department store and the Kremlin wall. The line is formidable, but it is kept moving right along by a well-placed gauntlet of boy soldiers wearing the solemn expressions of the churched, for Lenin's resting place is treated as a hallowed site.

Barry and I shuffle along with the admixture of tourists and Russian nationals. The closer we come to the mausoleum, the graver the expressions become. Upon approaching the door, even a whisper is curbed by the harsh "Ssshhhh!!" of the guards.

The chamber is dark and climate controlled. Lenin himself is immediately visible, lying in his glass sarcophagus, his unusually small head illuminated like the sea urchin lamps one sees in the cheap gift shops of boardwalk towns. A few paces ahead of me an American boy of about eleven makes a comment to his parents. A guard is immediately upon him. "Ssshhhh!!" This is ridiculous. After all, there is a gym for the honor guards in the tomb's basement. It is hard to maintain an air of solemnity when, beneath our feet, teenagers are doing push-ups, swigging vodka, and ogling dirty magazines.

We emerge from the tomb into the bright sunlight of the present day. "What did you think?" asks Barry.

My reply is immediate. "Bury him."

We return home toward evening. Igor is sitting at the kitchen table with Lena. He is smoking and she is cradling a teacup with both hands. As usual, they are happy to see us and treat us like long-lost kin. After we are fed—chicken with boiled potatoes—Igor takes Barry and me for a ride in his small car. We drive madly through the streets of Moscow, careening around corners and pedestrians. It is uphill all the way, into the smog-laden heavens, until, under a sky through which only the most determined stars wink, we arrive at a bluff in Moscow Heights. At the edge of the precipice is a monolithic marble railing, along which Russians sit, stand, smoke, and neck. The ground all about us is littered with cans, bottles, cigarette packs, and newspapers. Below us lies a basket of stars: Moscow itself.

"It's beautiful," I tell Igor.

He nods and puffs on his cigarette. "I have been in the great cities of the world," he reflects, "New York, Paris, London, Budapest, but I always come back to Moscow. This is the city I love. And I need nights like this to let me see all of it."

I make no reply to his statement. The contemplation of meeting my son in the morning has captured my thoughts. I wish I could honor Igor's musings with dutifully sensitive repartee, but I cannot. I need the space in my mind to let my thoughts and imaginings roam. I need this night as much as he does.

—— Wednesday, July 7, 1993 ——

After breakfast and saying good-bye to the ravens, Barry and I climb into Griescha's car in front of the apartment building. We take off with a lurch.

Nellie is riding up front with Griescha, chatting with him machine-gun fashion in Russian. The language hurries along so briskly that I am never sure whether a problem is afoot; the tongue sounds urgent by nature.

We are following another car, driven by Pavel, another one of Nellie's drivers. He speaks no English at all, not even Griescha's primitive "Okay!" A few blocks from the apartment both cars pull over. Nellie leans over the back of her seat. "We have to pick up Babs and Rick," she tells us.

Barry and I glance at one another, grateful that our car is already full.

Five, ten, fifteen minutes pass. Barry and I are anxious. We are going to see our kids today and those two can't even be on time for this momentous occasion! I cannot help but take this personally. Finally, Nellie alights from the car and goes to fetch them. Five minutes later she returns with the two of them in tow, Rick loudly complaining about something or other and Babs, smiling broadly and waving to Barry and me, furiously combing her hair while trying to hang onto an open bag of popcorn. For a moment the two of them surge toward our car and my heart sinks. Then Nellie redirects them toward Pavel and I well with sympathy for the man. I realize that even though he does not speak English, this will not daunt Babs. She will be his constant companion in conversation, lopsided though it be.

We are off. But ten minutes later we make another unannounced stop, on another busy street, outside another apartment building. Once again, we wait. After five minutes I can no longer stand the suspense. I ask Nellie what we are waiting for. Her reply is "Ada," only I do not know if this is a person or a thing. Then an older, white-haired woman comes out of the building. For reasons unknown, Nellie gets out of our car, admits Ada, and joins Babs and Rick in Pavel's car. I turn to Barry and ask, "Is it something we said?"

Our tiny caravan of small, wiperless cars moves out into the madness of Moscow's traffic. We then head out of the city on one of the highways. A minute later there is a sign: "Tula." Our car makes a graceful arc onto a right-hand spur, as if drawn there by gravity. Two hours, there are only two hours now.

I avail myself of the opportunity to see some of the Russian countryside. It is lovely in an ungroomed sort of way. In the States all the open fields belong to somebody and they are all mowed to the forest's edge, like nature's great green lawn. But the Russia I see is largely overgrown, like a house from which the owner has been away for ages. The highway passes through poor, unattractive villages, the tiny houses peelpaint, their timbers warped. Dusty, wan-looking children run through the streets or lean from windows. My perception is of a landscape slowly being subsumed into an environment of general decay—the Landscape of Usher.

The highway itself is constructed from what must be cheap concrete laid down in slabs like a sidewalk. Weeds grow in the cracks and the road is largely unadorned with lamps or services. It is simply a crumbling concrete path reaching out to infinity.

My heart quickens as I sense the imminence of civilization: more traffic, dirtier air, functional gas stations. We are again in the thick of it. A city, not unattractive at all. The feel is of Old Europe, with ornate façades, onion-domed churches, and a streetcar zipping down the main boulevard. Nellie explains to me that Tula was a closed city during the Soviet years. "They made munitions here," she adds. "Closed" means that even Soviet citizens who were not residents of Tula could not enter the place. The exclusion of tourists has left the city Russian, lovely, and old.

We pull into a driveway leading up to a red brick building. It looks like an old American-style public school. "Is Alyosha here?" I ask, already wriggling out of my cockpit. Nellie explains that this is the orphanage for the youngest children. "Infants to age five," she says. "We'll see Barry's little girl here and the kids Babs and Rick are adopting."

A large woman of about seventy greets us at the door. She is wearing a white clinical coat and a cylindrical white hat reminiscent of a chef. All this whiteness sets her blaze-red lipstick off to startling effect. "This is Ludmila," says Nellie. "She's in charge."

Ludmila: a thick, heavy, Russian name; wall-like; cold molasses; piano movers. We learn that she is a physician and was once very prominent and influential in the government. Ludmila speaks only Russian.

All of us have escaped from the cars now. We mill about, taking in the building, the playground that is knee-deep in weeds, and the immense, ancient sycamores whose far-reaching branches move only grudgingly in the cool breeze. When we enter the building there is a rush of activity: women younger than Ludmila, also in white, slipping in and out of doors and corridors in houseshoes. The interior of the orphanage is clean, but simple and furnished with only the essentials. Nellie leads Barry away in one direction, while Babs and Rick follow Ada in the other. I opt to go with Barry, running to catch up. "This is unreal," he says. "No," I answer. "This is it. This is real." I cannot believe that only weeks ago I was involved in an unholy relationship with Marilyn.

Barry and I follow Nellie into a large playroom that, prior to the Bolshevik Revolution, must have been the dining room or drawing room of some wealthy

Russian family. Now it is furnished with a few simple toys and populated by about twenty toddlers.

I must get a grip on the fact of my being here. Because orphanages have long been abolished in America, I sense that I have gone back in time. I look at the tiny boys and girls, heads sheared, uttering barely a sound. Two are playing on the floor with baubles, another is on a rocking horse, three others are simply sitting, waiting for nothing in particular. A little blond-haired boy of about two toddles up to me and extends his arms, saying *"Dya-dya"* ("Man"). I pick him up and he hugs my neck. "He's chosen you," laughs Nellie.

I look at her but cannot even force a smile. "Don't do that to me," I say, making an attempt to resist becoming attached to these little ones. I realize that in a minute I must put this child down and that I will never pick him up or see him again.

"His name is Nikolai," says Nellie.

"Put a hold on him," I tell her as I set him down on the floor. "In case I get a hankering for a second."

Barry and I are standing almost shoulder-to-shoulder, as if physically holding one another up. A white-clad woman comes through a corridor holding a little girl who is teary-eyed, her lower lip quivering. I look at my friend. "Barry, is this your daughter?"

Barry steps forward and holds up the little doll he has brought along. "This is Katya," says Nellie, presenting the child. Barry tries to get near her, but when he does Katya wails and the tears commence in earnest. "She's so scared," says Barry.

"She's never seen a man before," says Nellie, "especially one with a beard."

Eventually the caretaker succeeds in passing the child to Barry. She is inconsolable. Barry strokes her hair, whispers to her. He is led into a room, where he sits down with his daughter and rocks her, continuing to speak softly to her. A few minutes later she calms to a whimper, but remains perched on the brink of tears, ready to let go at the next unexpected move.

I leave Barry alone in the room so that he may commune with his daughter and his own thoughts in peace. Nellie approaches. "Let's see how Babs and Rick are making out," she says.

We head through a long corridor to another part of the building. No sooner do we enter the playroom there than I catch sight of Babs. Her son has just been brought in and... Oh, my God! It's Misha! She and Rick are adopting the child I passed over! I feel as if I have commended his soul to the deep. I watch as Babs tears at the boy, alternately shoving him away and yanking him toward her, crying "Mama! Mama! Mama!" in a braying, hee-haw fashion as she points to herself.

As I look on, Rick approaches me and begins to describe the workings of his camera, seemingly oblivious to the moment. "Have you met your son yet?" I ask him. Rick cracks a weak smile and continues to hang on the periphery while Babs proceeds to yo-yo Misha, his head whipping about like a rag doll. Babs looks at me and I can see the desperation in her eyes. She has wanted to be a mother with all her heart and all her soul for so long. Now she is letting it all hang out. She cannot help herself. She needs to touch someone, and since Rick is not available she is doing double-duty on Misha. As with Barry, I want to leave her alone while she is emoting. But before I do, I reach out and touch Misha on the cheek. *"Da sveedanya,"* I whisper.

I return to the wing where Barry has fallen in love with his daughter. One of the white-clad women signals that it is time for the children to eat. Barry reluctantly puts Katya down and she toddles over to an area of the playroom where several child-size table and chairs have been set up. The children take their places and allow the women to affix their bibs and spread them out on the table. The women set steaming bowls of soup on top of the bibs. Then, with a spoon in one hand and a chunk of bread in the other, these tiniest children begin to eat, rhythmically, in abject silence. It is like a monastic refectory minus the scripture readings. After the meal the children rise from their places and march into an adjoining room where they retrieve enamel pots. They drop their drawers and, in synchrony, do what has to be done. Then they go into their bedroom, undress, and turn in for their naps. I attribute all of this cooperation and civility to the absence of television.

Barry and Nellie join me out in the corridor. Babs and Rick show up a moment later. After Misha, she and Rick had visited their new infant daughter. Babs is spent. Her lava of love having flowed, she is, for the moment at least, the quiescent volcano.

"She was sleeping," says Babs, "so we couldn't disturb her." It is a blessing, for the baby could not possibly have survived the rattling Babs gave Misha.

We all pause for a deep breath. "Alyosha is a few miles from here," Nellie tells me. "It's your turn now."

I do not know if I am emotionally exhausted or emotionally charged from participating in Barry's and Babs's experiences. But ready or not, I know I must see Alyosha. There is no question of any delay, even for a cup of tea. Yes, Nellie has it exactly right: It is my turn now.

I can tell that Barry is reluctant to leave his little girl, yet he wants to be with me when I meet Alyosha for the first time. We reconstitute our caravan and set off under a thickening cloud cover and increasingly brisk winds, driving out of the city into the countryside. After a short while we come to what looks to be a summer camp—wooden lodgelike buildings surrounded by overgrown lots and wooden playhouses. "This is where they take the older kids in the summer," says Nellie as we park and alight. "To get them out in the fresh air."

I look around and see scatterings of boys running about, throwing us occasional, semi-interested glances. I grab my haversack, in which I have packed a handsome supply of chewing gum—a novelty in Russia. As we head down a footpath, two boys in their early teens pause and smile at me. I reach into my haversack and pull out a pack of gum for each of them. They accept the gift in a self-effacing manner, clasping my hand with both of theirs and saying, "*Spaseeba!*"

A bare mist of rain begins to make itself felt. The pendulous branches of silver maples and an occasional weeping willow sweep the still-dry ground. We arrive at one of the wooden lodges as our small group subconsciously reconfigures itself so that Nellie and I are moved to its apex. We enter the building and find ourselves standing in a sort of enclosed porch where not a soul is stirring. A door opens and a woman emerges. She is in her thirties; has brown, bobbed hair; and speaks only Russian. When Nellie identifies us she gives a slight bow and pulls her sweater more tightly about herself. Then she leaves us and opens a door on the far side of this porch, disappearing behind it.

I find myself standing alone in the middle of the floor, hovering apprehensively. The others have slowly withdrawn to the periphery of this stage to allow me this moment, as I have allowed them theirs. A far door opens and I rise up on my toes. I gaze into the distance, as if by force of will alone I can materialize the boy of my dreams.

I have never begun any important venture
for which I felt adequately prepared.

It is not to be yet. The threshold remains undarkened and the door closes again. I fall back down onto my heels. "He must be sleeping," says Nellie. "Naps are good," I say.

The door opens again. This time a little boy scurries out. Blond and shirtless, I squint after him to see if this perhaps is Alyosha, afraid of me, running away even before I have had a chance to say hello to him. Before I can turn in supplication to Nellie, he has disappeared into another room. "That wasn't him," she says. "That was Maxim."

A thought now strikes me for the first time. How will I greet my son? Should I hug him? What about a kiss? He is seven, though. Not a baby anymore. Would touching him scare him off? What if he won't come near me? What if? . . .

Circumstances have upended me. I no longer have the luxury of contemplation. Time has run out. The door is open and a little boy in blue shorts, blue shirt, and socks is being led out by the brown-haired woman. His head is bent and he is rubbing the sleep from his eyes. I wonder if I am going to cry, although I do not sense the proximity of tears. As Alyosha is brought to me, I become abruptly unaware of the presence of the world at large. It is as if all of existence has contracted to enclose only me and my son, who is lovelier in aspect than I could have imagined. I cannot believe that Russia is parting with this child. I kneel down before him and reach out. He looks up at me and puts his small hand in mine. It is so warm. His fingers are soft and slender—clarinetist's hands.

"Do you know who this is?" asks Nellie in Russian over my shoulder.

I am startled, not by the nature of the question but because I had forgotten that there was anyone in the room besides me and Alyosha. Without hesitation, but with the slightest sense of "What took you so long?", Alyosha looks into my eyes and asks, "Papa?"

It is at this point that I brace my lip for the first time. I reach up and touch his full cheek. Yes, this is really him . . . in the flesh. I dig down into my haversack and retrieve a small gift: a Pez dispenser styled as a toy truck. I hand it to Alyosha, who is fascinated with it, smiling brightly as he turns it around in his hands, his delicate fingers exploring every niche and line. I show him how to open it to insert the candy. He catches on immediately. This is a sure sign of intelligence, because Pez dispensers are notoriously difficult to load.

Make this moment last, I tell myself. Make it last, for he is more precious now than he will ever be, because you can touch him, but you cannot have him yet. I pull out a small photo album. It contains pictures of me, my house, my family, my pickup truck, my canoe. There is also a picture of Alyosha's school, unremarkable because it was taken before it went on alert. With the help of a Russian friend, I have written captions in Alyosha's language: "Our House," "Our Canoe," "My Mother and Father/Your Grandma and Grandpa." Alyosha reads all of them aloud. I search his blue eyes for the quality of his response. Does all this overwhelm him? Does he know he will be leaving Russia to live with me in America? Has he ever heard of America?

"Nellie," I say, summoning her to my side. "Ask Alyosha what he knows about America."

She asks, and his reply is almost immediate: "I will have all the bubblegum I want."

During this time several of the other boys in Alyosha's room have been trying to sneak out to see what is going on. Each time, though, the brown-haired woman hurries over, stuffs them back inside, and closes the door. But now they have made good their escape, and six of them crowd around me and Alyosha, craning their necks to see the photo album, wondering at the Pez dispenser. Their smiles are genuine, but their expressions also contain the recognition of what is going on here: they are losing a member of their ranks. He is going to America and they will never see him again. The brown-haired woman begins to flank them like a border collie, shooing them back into their room. But it is no use: they are free and they outnumber her.

Nellie suggests that we go for a walk. Alyosha takes me to his room, which sleeps eight boys. He puts on his ill-fitting, worn shirt and pants, torn sneakers, and an old, threadbare poplin coat. Then he takes my hand and we are on our way. He has not run away from me after all. I think he really wants me to be his. I keep looking down at him as we walk along. He keeps looking up at me. Sometimes our eyes meet. When they do, he beams—a smile that illuminates his entire face.

I feel as if we are taking some kind of inaugural walk, leading an entourage consisting of Barry, the Duluths, Nellie, and Ada, as well as a smattering of shirtless and barefoot boys. I ask Nellie about their prospects for adoption. "Most of them are too old," she tells me.

"Too old?"

"When they turn nine, the government no longer tries to find families for them because so few want an older child. So the resources are concentrated on getting the younger ones adopted."

Alyosha is seven. It is painful to consider that had no one wanted him he might have remained without a family for the rest of his childhood. "What happens to the kids who don't get adopted?" I ask.

"They stay in the system, are educated, and at sixteen are apprenticed in various trades." It sounds like something out of Dickens. Yet the foster-care system in the States cannot guarantee even this degree of attention.

Alyosha breaks away from me and runs over to a log playhouse on stilts. He clambers up into it, calls out to me, and I applaud his accomplishment. He climbs like a monkey. Then, from the seven-foot height, he threatens to jump. "No," I tell him, signaling dramatically. "Climb down." But he laughs and jumps anyway, springing to the ground and throwing his arms up in a gesture of victory.

Alyosha sees one of the other boys standing close to me. He runs over and scoops up my hand again, nudging the other aside. Alyosha has never owned anything in his life, and all of a sudden he has been presented with a six-foot-three-inch American. His possessiveness is understandable.

Nellie suggests that we have Alyosha's passport photo taken while we are in Tula. Griescha drives us into the city with Alyosha sitting on my lap. I love his closeness, his weight, his hand resting in mine. With my nose buried in his neck, I consider the weight of his culture as well: the large, gracious women who have cared for him in the orphanage; the aromatic Russian foods; and the impossible, expressive, explosive Russian language that for the moment stands between us like a wall but despite which we see one another so clearly.

The photography studio is dark and silent, with four or five customers standing grimly in line awaiting the cue of the photographer. When it is Alyosha's turn to enter the chamber, I follow him. He is told to look forward and lift his head; there is no summons to smile. This small act of having his picture taken is another indication to me that this adoption will take place, despite the amount of paperwork that lies ahead and the signatures of approval that must still be obtained. It is as if in casting his image on paper—truly a magical act—I am conjuring the future as well.

Late in the afternoon we take Alyosha back. I harbor a degree of resentment about this, as if I am commending him to orphanage existence when our compatibility has already been established and he has already trespassed the boundaries of his institutional world in my care. We alight from the cars and the brown-haired woman steps forward to take Alyosha back. I ask Nellie to translate to him. "Tell him I'll be back for him in a week," I say. Alyosha nods. "And ask him if he'll miss me."

Alyosha looks up at me. "I won't miss you," he answers thoughtfully, "but I'll wait for you."

I am impressed with this answer. It's different. Alyosha steps close and hugs me long and tight. Now I am close to tears. "Good-bye," I tell him. He surprises me by answering, "Good-bye." Someone in the crowd has snuck him his first English word.

We get into the cars and pull away. I wave to Alyosha until I can no longer see him. He is not even mine yet and already I cannot imagine life without him.

—— Thursday, July 8, 1993 ——

As Robert Penn Warren said, "There's always something."

We are back in the apartment in Moscow when Nellie calls. She has dropped a bombshell. In order for the adoption to proceed the head of the oblast, or provincial region, in which Tula lies must sign the necessary papers. But he has refused. It seems that a letter to the editor has appeared in one of the newspapers, questioning the whole concept of the foreign adoption of Russian children. This has sent the entire process into a tailspin.

"But I thought Alyosha was preapproved," I argue.

"This is different," explains Nellie, quietly and clearly. Barry is sitting at the kitchen table, his eyes wide with alarm. "The head of the oblast is scared. He's new and doesn't want to do anything politically unwise."

"What does this mean?" I beg. "That the adoption is off?" When I say this Barry all but tears the phone out of my hands.

"I don't think there will be a problem," says Nellie. "He wants to appoint a committee to come up with a new policy for him on the issue of adoption in his district."

"A committee!" I exclaim. In the States a committee is a prelude to an eternity of indecision. What must it mean in notoriously bureaucratic Russia? This is a country where government officials still count with the abacus—a powerful symbol of the state of efficiency in this part of the world. "Nellie," I argue, "I've got to get out of Russia in ten days. Do you really think Russian law is going to be rewritten by then?"

Nellie continues to beg for our patience and understanding. "Ludmila is on our side," she says. "She has powerful influence."

Barry is breathing down my neck. "Ludmila is on our side," I repeat to him, and he eases off a bit.

Nellie advises us to sit tight and not to worry. She offers to take me to the Chekhov museum. "I feel as if I should be doing something in my own interest," I tell her, "to strengthen my case."

"There's nothing you can do, except go to the Chekhov museum."

I hang up and tell Barry what has happened. He is incredulous. We can do nothing more than acknowledge our powerlessness and commiserate. I want to tell Nellie that I have my rights, until it dawns on me that here, in Russia, I do not have my rights. I want to complain to the person in charge, but soberly concede that this is probably impossible. Barry decides to call his wife in the States. "Wait'll she hears this!" he says grimly. "She'll be furious. She'll call Donna."

"Good," I tell him, "we need all the help we can get," although I am not sure that pressure exerted from that quarter will abet our cause. But this consideration is moot, because Barry cannot get through. We vent our frustration and anger for another few minutes, and then each of us deals with the situation in his own way: Barry retreats to his room to be alone and I head out to the Chekhov museum to take my mind off things.

Chekhov is far and away my favorite Russian author and one of my favorite authors overall. Stepping into his house does transport me. In that place so charged with his memory, I am, indeed, better able to rationalize my circumstances: all will be well and all is well. This is just a temporary delay.

The Chekhov museum is housed in the writer's home. At the entrance sits an old babushka in a glass booth. She charges Nellie the Russian admission price of about sixty cents, while I am required to pay ten times that much. I bristle at this. I expect this woman to know what I am going through and I want to be accorded an appropriate degree of latitude and mercy. But she looks so formidable—short and square with thick, red, chapped hands—that I am sure I would be no match for her, especially in a haggle over ticket prices.

Except for Nellie and me, the museum is vacant of other visitors. Still, almost every room contains another vigilant babushka in housecoat and slippers, seated in a corner, waiting, watching for the least faux pas.

Before we enter the first room with its polished parquet floor, we are required to put on felt-soled overshoes that tie around the ankles. Nellie's tiny feet are well-contained within the things, but I cannot find a pair quite large enough for mine. Every time I lift my feet they fly off, and a babushka rises from her seat and begins hurling recriminations at me. The result is that I must shuffle along without raising my feet from the floor. This presents a special problem when ascending the interior staircase—to keep the overshoes on my feet I must scrape the toe up the riser of each step. This makes the entire museum visit a labor. I find that I can either study the exhibits or keep my overshoes on; I cannot do both. Whenever I try to it is the overshoe that fails and I find myself under attack by a babushka.

Even in these hallowed rooms, with their Victorian furniture and crystal chandeliers, the placards describing aspects of Chekhov's life, his medical tools spread out on a work desk, I find my thoughts drifting back to Tula. I am constantly wondering what Alyosha is doing at the moment.

"The thing is," I tell Nellie out of the blue, "my airline tickets are fixed. I can't change them. If I don't fly out of here on the eighteenth I will lose them. And, Nellie, I can't afford to lose them. I'm at the end of my money. What if? . . ."

"If you don't get Alyosha by the eighteenth?"

I nod.

"Then it may be necessary to have him escorted to the States."

I am not as alarmed as I feel I should be by this eventuality. Within Nellie's statement is contained her belief that, by hook or by crook and in a timely manner or not, Alyosha will become my son.

"It's not time to worry yet," she repeats. "We're checking on the situation every day."

As we move toward the exit of the museum one of my overshoes comes off, unbeknownst to me. A leathery babushka cries out. I look at her and shake my head, as if to reprimand her. I can feel my limits of tolerance contracting. I have become easily annoyed. I feel as if a good fight, a physical fight, is just what I need. But not with the babushka.

I stop at a small gift booth and admire some sepia-toned photographs of Chekhov. Nellie tells me they are twenty-five rubles for Russians—about two and a half cents—for a set of four. The price for foreigners is several dollars. "Nellie," I say, "I want all four photos, but for the Russian price."

Perhaps struck by the gravity of my tone, Nellie goes to work at once while I drift away from her to avoid contaminating the effort. A moment later she comes up to me with the photos—at the Russian price. As we leave the museum I am flush with victory. I needed this small concession. I feel as if I have won the physical fight I was looking for.

On the way back to Potapovsky Prospect I ask Nellie if there is somewhere I can buy Russian children's books. She takes me to a department store. Until recently there were interminable queues for everything in Moscow; these have been replaced by unruly mobs. The one at the book counter is particularly formidable. It takes me fifteen minutes to slug my way through to the front, with Nellie in tow. I pick out a Russian-English picture dictionary for children. When I try to carry the book away, there is an outcry on the part of the employees. Nellie takes me by the arm. "No," she says, "this is where you simply make your selection. Over there," she explains, pointing to another mob in another part of the store, "is where you pay for the book. But you can't have it until you pay for it."

I dutifully retrieve a slip from the book woman and take it over to the slugfest at the cashier. After ten minutes I have paid for the book. Then I carry my receipt back to the book counter, where after another fifteen minutes of world-class wrestling I have the book in hand. It has taken me only forty minutes to purchase a dictionary in which the plural of "tooth" is diligently rendered "tooths."

On the way home Nellie heroically tries to avoid the subject of the complications that have arisen with respect to the adoptions. I cannot. I explain to her that in the States I have always considered myself very capable in the area of not worrying about crises until they actually materialize. "But I feel out of control here," I tell her. "In the States I'm used to confronting difficulties and working to resolve them myself. But here I am forced to rely on other people, and this has made me feel powerless."

Nellie consoles me. "It's not time to panic," she advises yet again. I acknowledge this, although I feel that I have moved beyond panic and am flirting with despair. I just don't know what I will do with the days if there is no resolution in sight as my departure date draws nearer.

"Have you thought of going to the zoo?" asks Nellie, trying to be helpful.

That's just it: I feel as if I am already in the zoo. But I do not tell Nellie this. She is my best hope for success, and she is truly a good and caring person.

Nellie recommends that I try to take the metro home on my own. I seize this challenge as a much-needed diversion. I say good-bye to Nellie, buy my fragile tiddly-wink tokens, and board the train along with a thousand Muscovites. Ten minutes down the line I realize that I have boarded the wrong train. Should it continue east for a couple of days or so, I will be in Siberia.

There is always something.

Friday, July 9, 1993

The ravens arrived early this morning to squawk their harsh reveilles. Their cries are moot, for my night was a restless one. The tension induced by all this uncertainty has given me a headache. The pain attacked me where I lay, and now it has attached itself to me like an imp. It will pursue me through this day.

Barry and I sit at Lena's kitchen table, he with his coffee and I with my tea. The apprehension in the air is palpable. I am convinced that Lena senses it as well, yet she says nothing because her vocabulary is not up to the task. In any case, there is nothing she can say.

Barry and I begin to discuss the situation in a manner suggesting that we believe we can influence affairs. "There are five points I want to make to Nellie," I tell him, "if she has to go argue our cases." I go on to list these tenets, like a lawyer in a courtroom:

We were invited here by Russian government officials.
We are already in the country, at great expense.
We cannot stay away from our jobs indefinitely.
We have already met the children.
We have return air tickets for ourselves and the children.

I rattle off my piece with the faith of the true believer. What I do not consider is that the forces I feel myself aligned against are largely faceless and will, in all probability, remain so. I also have another regret: the current preoccupation has co-opted me from enjoying this culture. For this I feel great compunction. When I look at Lena I feel a double dose of it, for I want to avoid any word, gesture, or attitude that passes judgment on her country.

"Should we call Nellie?" Barry asks.

I tell him that if anything has changed she will undoubtedly call us. But that is not really his point. There is a surreal sense that if we do not remain in steady contact we will be forgotten. Barry attempts to call. After several tries, he hangs up. Once again the phone is out of order. "Maybe she *has* been trying to reach us," he says.

"Maybe we shouldn't even think about that. If she needs to get in touch with us, she'll do it."

We decide we cannot just sit and wait like condemned prisoners. We need to act as if there are no problems and we are going to adopt these kids. "Let's go shopping," I announce, words that taste as alien to me as borscht. Still, I would like to buy more books for Alyosha to seed his Russian library back in the States. "Is there anything you're looking for?" I ask Barry.

"Yeah. A potty seat, for when I get her back here."

I smile. This is exactly the kind of talk that puts heart into both of us. We need this illusion of creating our own futures.

If one does not patronize the impossibly crowded stores with the impolite help, shopping is not so nightmarish in Moscow. This is because Russia has not simply accepted the capitalist manifesto, it has embraced it with gusto. Nellie has told us that not long ago a law was passed permitting anybody to sell anything anywhere anytime, no holds barred. The result has been an explosive entrepreneurship that has made all of Moscow a mercantile commons.

Barry and I leave the apartment and walk down Potapovsky Prospect toward the Kremlin. It is not long before we are embraced by a vigorous, cacophonous midway of kiosks and card tables. If the barkers are not hawking from their stalls, they are stalking us on the street. Most of the consumers are Russians, newly possessed by a "shop 'til you drop" mentality fueled by an inflation rate of twenty-five percent that discourages saving. As I enter this frenzy, I immediately realize that I do not need a walk through the silent chambers of St. Basil's. What I need is the pandemonium of this bazaar to take my mind off things.

Barry and I move among the men, women, and children selling chewing gum, Mars bars, faucet washers, and the omnipresent shots of vodka. A tow-headed Russian boy of about twelve runs up to me. "Mister! Only five dollars!" he yells as he unfurls a chamois of sports and political pins—great favorites here—and with his free hand reflexively brushes the hair from his eyes.

"*Nyet, spaseeba,*" I say with practiced fluency.

"Please!" he begs as I walk along and he backsteps to maintain his wares before my eyes.

"*Nyet, nyet,*" I repeat. Then, in a final frontal assault, he pleads, "For your son!" I pause and look at him. He does not understand that I have come here to forget about the absence of that very fact. "*Nyet,*" I say softly, apologetically. The boy senses the tenor of my message and runs off to greener pastures.

No sooner do we resume our walk than it is Barry who is under assault. He is dealing with a middle-aged woman who, astonishingly, has thrust a potty seat before him. Barry buys it for two dollars. Completely satisfied, he sticks it under his arm and we continue on.

This is capitalism unbridled, laissez-faire taken to heart. I am convinced that the woman set out this morning convinced she would sell the potty seat. The impulse to buy has become reflexive, stimulated by a flood of once-rare imports. As I watch the manic acts of shopping taking place before my eyes, I am amazed that even the elderly are not daunted by such exertions. Perhaps after years of waiting in interminable lines the task of muscling one's way to a kiosk is invigorating to the average Russian. But I would have to be hell-bent on having something, as was the case with the book of tooths, to justify struggling through a crowd of Muscovites pressing forward with fistfuls of fragile rubles.

This new commercial freedom has made Moscow a very busy city. I cannot help feeling compelled to move, to go with the flow, because around the next corner may be someone with something I wish to buy. And by jingo, there she is: a woman selling children's books from a folding table. I approach and begin to handle her wares, but she is neither affable nor accommodating. No matter how carefully I replace a book I have examined, she straightens it with a disgust that seems to say, "So! You didn't want it? Well, either move aside or buy—you're disturbing those with money!"

I finally do purchase a lovely hardcover book of fairy tales for three hundred rubles—thirty cents. I hand the woman a five-hundred-ruble note, but even this has irritated her, for it results in a delay. She digs through her shoebox and finally gives me my change: two hundred rubles and no *spaseeba.*

Barry and I walk on. Ten minutes later we pause to take a breather and lean up against a wall. The next thing I know I am surrounded by six people asking what I am selling. I throw up my hands and they retreat in disgust. I have upended them, cost them time; and time, as every Russian has newly learned, is money.

It is not long before the bazaar has become too much. We decide to head for more placid environs, but this means having to cross the street. The horrendous traffic situation contributes to the agony of the commons in Moscow. It is dense, random, and deadly. Because most of the streets have no painted lines and motor vehicles have the right of way, the street corners are jammed with huddles of people surging and retreating in turn as they probe the speeding phalanxes of boxy, sputtering Ladas for openings to enable them to cross. As Barry and I stand waiting with the other hopefuls, a car peels out of the traffic and careers toward us on a collision course. My first impulse is to grab the potty seat and throw it at the vehicle as a symbolic counterattack. At the last moment the car stops, someone from the crowd gets in, and it skids away. This, I later learn, is a taxi, unmarked as most of them are, because anyone can call his car a taxi in Moscow. An outstretched arm at curbside may summon a frenzy of such freelancers, zig-zagging their way through the traffic, risking life and limb for the always-negotiable fare.

On the way home the street leading to Potapovsky Prospect seems to be thickening with activity, even though it is late in the day. A commotion erupts nearby. A police car, its siren wailing and lights flashing, is *backing* its way at high speed through dense traffic. Barry and I step back to avoid being hit as it pulls over to the curbside not ten feet from where we are standing. Two officers alight from the vehicle and muscle their way through the crowd. I lean over to Barry. "Someone's in for it!" But when I nose in through the sidewalk crowd to get a closer look at the scene of the crime, I see an old babushka selling Mars bars. The police have used their authority merely to get to the front of the mob. They have no intention of letting their jobs interfere with their duty: to buy.

Barry and I move on. This day has been well spent because we have simply managed to spend it. At breakfast I would not have imagined this possible. As Barry and I draw closer to the apartment building, closer to our timeworn street of leaning sycamores and crumbling façades, I grow reflective and even optimistic about this country's prospects. Somehow, some day, the ruble will be convertible, inflation will be reined in, traffic lines will be painted, and the ululations of hawkers will be confined to designated business zones. It will be a place to which I will return with my son. There. Having thought this, I have created yet another future. Between Barry's potty seat and my power to imagine, everything is going to be okay. Even my headache has vanished.

—— Saturday, July 10, 1993 ——

Once again I awake with a headache. Now I am convinced they are tension induced.

Nellie calls: still no word from the powers that be. "We are working on it," she tells us. Then there is a fragment of good news. Ludmila has done me the favor of picking up Alyosha's passport photos. I feel as if we have taken yet another step into the future I have defined for us.

Griescha has been suggesting for several days now that he be permitted to take Barry and me to a huge and famous flea market in Moscow called Izmailova. "They have everything," he says when he comes to the apartment to get us. I am startled by this pronouncement. It is the first English other than "Okay!" I have heard him speak.

Hanging onto the security straps of Griescha's car, we are whisked away toward what is reported to be the mother of all flea markets. Griescha's wild, antic driving alone is enough to make the time pass. We finally arrive at Izmailova. It *is* vast. In fact, it is a city unto itself, a literal maze of kiosks stretching off as far as the eye can see and spilling from its acreage onto surrounding city streets. Barry and I immediately begin to explore this bonfire of capitalist vanities. Griescha tells us that here the customer is expected to haggle over prices, but when I try to bargain for a handpainted wooden brooch I am rebuffed at the outset. In fact, the seller is so offended by my attempt that she refuses to do any business with me at all.

Barry has better luck. He is the quintessential disinterested buyer, and he manages to purchase a handful of T-shirts at a cut-rate price. "Barry," I tell him, "wouldn't it be ironic if we return home with suitcases full of souvenirs but no kids?" Barry casts a sharp look at me. My jibe flirts too freely with possibility to be ironic.

My one small shopping coup occurs when I spot a laminated map of Russia in a lean-to brimming with bric-a-brac. The old man wants two thousand five hundred rubles for it—$2.50—but I manage to get him down to two thousand even. He shrugs his shoulders, rolls the map up, and hands it to me. I need these small victories. I need to control trivial events to create the illusion of having any control at all.

Barry and I leave Izmailova with our arms full of gleanings: T-shirts, map, handpainted Christmas decorations, and handcarved jewelry boxes. We have been away from the apartment for four hours and therefore owe Griescha twelve dollars. He examines the money we hand him before pocketing it. He shakes our hands with something resembling gratitude, and I am happy for having made someone else happy.

When we enter the apartment Lena tells us that Nellie has not called since we left. We had not expected her to, but Lena's announcement is nonetheless disconcerting. It reminds me that my plane tickets are good for only eight more days. For a moment I panic. My God, what can possibly be accomplished in eight days? How can a committee be formed and render a decision on something so momentous as adoption policy for an entire province in just eight days?

This thought pursues me through late afternoon and into the evening. By 11:00 P.M. my mind settles on something I had forgotten: the blatt. I have a whole bag of it sitting in my room. Perhaps I can launch a preemptive blatt campaign to jolt the adoption authorities to action. I lie down in bed, but this idea has such appeal to me that I find myself fighting a rising inclination to drift off to sleep. I am exhausted. Only I am not sure if it is the exhaustion of exploring Izmailova for four hours or the exhaustion engendered by a slowly burgeoning resignation: I am not going to take Alyosha home with me. I must return home alone, for the moment, anyway. It is as simple as that. I am being unrealistic in expecting a miracle. Nellie is as powerless as I am in this. It is over, then. My head begins to swim with these thoughts. I find myself being pulled down into sleep, as if something has its hands on me and is gently but persistently imploring me to let go, let go. I finally do relinquish my hold on the day, and the balcony window goes black.

— Sunday, July 11, 1993 —

There is no activity on the adoption front, but the domestic rhythms of my life here have been disrupted. Lena and Igor have announced that they are going on vacation. "But what about us?" I ask for Barry and me, the way a seven year old would.

"No worry," says Lena with a wave of her hand. "My mother will take care of you." An hour later she and Igor are gone and I do not know when I will see them again.

The day is gloomy: cool, windy, and with a low cloud cover. So Barry and I mull around the apartment. We play chess. We read John Grisham novels. We are like an old expatriate married couple living in Moscow, of all places. Nellie is supposed to call sometime today, but we do not know when. I consider for a moment how small and uncomplicated my life has become when the value I assign my existence is predicated on someone else's giving me a ring.

As morning drags on toward noon, both Barry and I grow hungry. I become slightly alarmed. My goodness, who will cook for us if the mother doesn't show up? How dependent we have become. There are some crackers in a bowl on the table, but they will not last forever, and there is a cabbage in the cupboard large enough to feed the population of the Kamchatka Peninsula. Then, as if on cue, the mother appears at noon. She is a big-boned woman of about seventy wearing a faded housecoat and fuzzy bedroom slippers. Her gray hair is coiled into a neat bun and she wears thick, thick glasses. She pours forth a torrent of Russian upon seeing us. Her language is matter-of-fact and precipitous, as if she has known us all her life and we understand every word she says. She runs to the stove with the hurried deliberation of the born cook. While talking to us over her shoulder, she begins to shuffle pots and pans and utensils. Hot dog, we are going to be fed again.

We never learn this woman's name. I come to think of her as our babushka. I learn not to fear her attempts at communication, because she seems satisfied with our blank expressions of incomprehension.

Barry and I sit at the kitchen table like customers in a restaurant. Our patience is rewarded with two heaping platters of those pancakes the size of silver dollars. Then comes a round of sausage, and eggs, and bread, and finally soup. Barry rolls his hand over his belly, looks up at me, and slowly shakes his head. It is much too much food. "We have to eat it," I urge him. "Out of respect."

Barry digs in. I dig in. I finish the egg, a piece of sausage, and five of the pancakes. I still have a good sixteen more on my plate. Taken by a schoolboyish impulse to let loose, I tell Barry there is a strange bird on the windowsill. When he turns to look at it I transfer three of my pancakes to his plate. This goes on every few minutes. "Barry," I say, "Do you think those are rain clouds?" He turns, he looks, and I load his plate again. Finally the babushka is standing over my empty plate, wringing her hands with joy. A gentle tear slips from her left eye. When she looks at Barry, though, she clucks her tongue, because his plate contains the Leaning Tower of Pancakes. "Oh, Barry," I rebuke him, "you've insulted her."

Barry throws up his hands. "I can't seem to put a dent in them," he says.

Unfortunately I get my comeuppance for the ploy. My performance has pleased the babushka too well, for she loads my plate with yet another mound of pancakes. But it is impossible, simply impossible to eat another morsel. When the babushka excuses herself to go to the bathroom, I grab the plate, hurry to my room, open the balcony doors, and feed the pancakes to the ravens. They are grateful for the repast, their greedy ruckus loud enough to raise the dead.

After lunch Barry and I retreat to our rooms to nap. We arise at 2:00 P.M., our biological clocks in perfect synchrony, and find tea and cakes awaiting us in the kitchen. Barry attempts to tell the babushka that he drinks coffee. But she only pours him more tea, which he dutifully sips, this seeming to be the path of least resistance.

After our tea we talk for a while and then retreat to our rooms once again. I read some more John Grisham. I roll over on the bed and observe the increased number of ravens perched on the balcony railing. After only one feeding of the babushka's pancakes, the word has apparently spread. Before I know it I have drifted off to sleep once again. At 4:30 P.M. there is more food, after which I sleep. At 9:00 the babushka serves us cabbage soup and bread and sliced cucumbers. Then I go back to my room, read, and lull in bed, willing sleep to take me.

I realize that I am approaching that state of mind Lena spoke about early on: having a life that one hates. Perhaps that means I am supposed to love

Russia as a sort of counterbalance to that self-destructive feeling. But I do not. I simply wish I had more reason to enjoy being where I am. Nellie could give me that reason. If only she would call as she said she would. What frightens me is that I am beginning, just beginning, not to care whether she calls or not. My sleeping and eating and hovering has made me feel unwashed, out of shape, useless. I feel as if I have contracted a chronic disease. Then I become angry with myself for indulging in self-pity. I decide to regard this day as the low point of my stay in Russia.

I convert the seven days remaining to me into 168 hours. Now it sounds as if a lot of time remains in which this adoption can be completed. I am becoming good at illusion, something that I have always believed in anyway. "If you don't like a book," one of my high-school English teachers once told me, "just make believe it's interesting and you're bound to find that it really is." How true, how true. It was this philosophy that helped me ply the pages of *Ivanhoe* to the last. This conjuring of few days into many hours will also work. I am convinced of it. As proof of the peace this conviction affords me, I fall right to sleep.

Monday, July 12, 1993

I have entered the week when things *must* start to happen.

But how can anything be accomplished in six days? I do not have Alyosha's passport, his visa, or his physical. But first things first: I must get Alyosha.

Barry and I have breakfast together. We watch CNN on television as the babushka cooks her heart out for us. Every so often she peers at us through those lenses that swell her eyes to gigantic proportions, like the comic glasses worn by Ernie Kovacs. Before we know what is happening she is shoveling her tiny pancakes onto our plates again. Barry girds himself for the descent into the doughy mound. I distract him to imaginary sights outside the window so that I can load his plate with half of mine. Then I get up, go to my room, and feed the rest to the ravens. I return to the kitchen, have tea, chat, look at the phone, thank the babushka, and sleep until noon. This lethargic, aimless lifestyle reminds me of the lyric sung by the inhabitants of the Emerald City of Oz:

> We get up at twelve and start to work at one,
> Take an hour for lunch and then at two we're done,
> Jolly good fun!

Only this is not jolly good fun. It is torment. "This dead time is killing me," I tell Barry. Truly, I do not understand why all the paperwork was not done before we arrived in Russia. "Why did they wait until we got here before attempting to get all of the signatures we needed?"

Barry is mute on this. He commiserates, but I see that even complaining aloud is losing its power to mollify either of us.

Toward 10:00 P.M.—after a day spent as wastrels—Nellie calls. Her voice spills over the line in a wash of static. She tells us that the special commission on adoption has acted in our favor. "They have given their approval."

My heart leaps. "Then it's a done deal?" I say. "I mean, we can take these kids home?"

"No, the commission has made only a recommendation, which has been forwarded to the head of the oblast," says Nellie. "He must now decide whether to sign the forms permitting the adoption to proceed."

"Where are these papers?" I ask.

"On his desk. All we need now is his signature. We're confident that we'll get it."

I was right. Yesterday *was* the low point of this experience. The news of the commission's approval is light at the end of the tunnel. Barry and I sit up late talking. For the past several days our conversations have seemed stuck in time: ruminations about our sorry situation, bitter appraisals of the way we are being handled. But now we are once again able to consider the future. It is as if we have been fighting a long war and there is now talk of victory and peace. We are like two old soldiers in a foxhole during a lull in the shooting. One turns to the other and asks, "What will you do when it's really over?" The other reflects for a moment and says, "I'm gonna get me a pizza."

Yes, that sounds good to me too, grammar and all. I'm gonna get me and Alyosha a pizza so he can have his first big bite of America.

—— Tuesday, July 13, 1993 ——

It is a dreary day, an empty day. Barry and I go with Nellie to a store called "Children's World," where Barry fights for his life to get to the head of a mob in an attempt to find shoes for his daughter. He succeeds in buying a pair of leather sandals for about fifty cents. I try to get Alyosha a pair of sneakers, but it is no go. The salespeople are too dour and aggressive. Nellie is barely finished intoning the request when, with eyes averted, the young woman behind the counter is snapping *"Nyet, nyet, nyet."* I ask Nellie why the answer is always no. "They probably do have the shoes," she explains, "but after so many years of shortages they say no out of habit."

After the enervation of our shopping trip Barry and I return to the apartment, have tea, chat, and lounge around. Barry complains that he seems to be getting fat. This is interesting to me, for I have noticed that the ravens are becoming heavier as well—and all this since the arrival of the babushka. However, my six-foot-three frame is holding steady at a slim 175 pounds.

Nellie calls very late. "Tomorrow we go to Tula to pick up the children."

Barry and I are ecstatic. "So the papers have been signed?"

"We assume so," says Nellie. "We can't reach the head of the oblast by phone, but he's had the papers on his desk for a couple of days now and he knows we want to pick up the kids, so they must be signed."

Yes, they must be signed.

—— Wednesday, July 14, 1993 ——

Nothing.

Nellie calls and tells us that we will not be going to Tula today. The papers have not been signed. I remind her that my appointment at the embassy is in two days. "What am I going to do?" I plead, near panic.

"Can you change your plane ticket?"

"That's just it. I can't change my tickets. In four days I must fly out of Russia."

It has gotten worse, then. Overnight everything seems to have changed. "I thought you said that the papers were on this man's desk."

"Yes," Nellie says. "But we called Tula this morning and he has gone on vacation."

"Can't someone else sign the papers then?" I reason. "Doesn't he have a deputy of some sort?"

It is here that I learn a lesson about the Russian bureaucracy and how it differs from our own. In Russia, authority is so coveted that it is never delegated. The possessor of authority takes it with him wherever he goes—on vacation, to the hospital, abroad. I presume that he takes it to the grave as well. Despite this insight, I am enraged that this man chose to go to his *dacha* when all we needed was a brief flourish of his pen. "I just can't believe it," I tell Nellie. "What on earth are we going to do now?"

"Tomorrow we go to Tula," she says. "We have to go. Just don't worry."

I am beyond worry. I am now mired in despair.

Thursday, July 15, 1993

Once again the cars are called upon to take Babs, Rick, Barry, and me to Tula. I have packed a change of clothes for Alyosha and taken my plastic bag of blatt along, although I am not at all convinced that receiving Alyosha is a given. Nellie will not be joining us on this trip, which I find disconcerting. Instead, Ada accompanies us as our noble, hopeful band heads south over the same broken highway, past the same blown-out gas stations, and through the same ungroomed, overgrown countryside. We arrive in Tula, where Ada goes straight to work. Although her face is careworn, when I observe her eyes I see a burning deliberation that puts heart into me.

We enter a modern-looking administration building—the seat of this province. Ada takes me with her to the fourth floor. I do not know why Barry and the Duluths have been left below. We enter an office remarkable for its lack of paperwork. There is a desk, a few books, and a typewriter. Finally, a buxom woman walks in. She is about fifty, wearing heavy makeup, with her brown hair teased up into a bouffant. She sits behind her desk and begins to peck at the manual typewriter. After a few moments she begins muttering, "Alyosha, Alyosha, Alyosha," without looking at either of us.

Ada begins to talk at her. The woman fires a paragraph back at Ada. I observe the duo with a mixture of awe and helplessness. All of a sudden someone murmurs the word "papa." The conversation ceases and the two women look at me, sitting on my hands in a wooden chair against the wall, my toes angled toward each other like a nine year old waiting to see the principal. I feel as if I am expected to speak, but I do not. Instead I do what probably should have been done at the outset. Reaching into my plastic bag and taking steady aim, I blatt this woman.

"Who is she?" I ask Ada after I have pushed a small jar of Maine blueberry honey across her desk.

"She is the woman who directly oversees adoptions in this province," she says.

"Is she powerful?"

Ada nods. "We must have her signature."

I reach into my plastic bag, pull out a bottle of skin lotion, and blatt her again.

The conversation erupts anew. Within moments the decibel level has increased to the point at which I would call it an argument. Hands go out, papers are thrown down on the desktop, and expressions register exasperation and disgust. My heart sinks. I turn to Ada in supplication, "It's not going to happen, is it?"

Ada calms me with a hand gesture. "Everything's okay," she says distractedly before descending into the fray again.

After a half hour in this office, the two women stand, congeal, and head out of the office as a unit with me and my plastic bag of blatt taking up the rear. We descend to the third floor, where we enter an office that is both bigger and better appointed. I am told to sit in another wooden chair against another wall. The two women enter the next room; the door closes behind them. Within moments a frightening din erupts. It sounds as if someone's heart is being torn out. A drawer slams. A fist strikes a desktop. Papers are riffled. A man's voice rises. Someone is being murdered and I am a witness to this crime.

Fifteen minutes of near hysteria go by. Then, suddenly, the voices fade and a period of calm sets in, during which I imagine a body being dragged behind a desk. Then the door opens and the women emerge. They look worse for wear. "My God, Ada, what went on in there?"

"Nothing," she says. "We got the signature we needed."

"From the head of the oblast? I thought he was on vacation."

"He was on vacation," she says. "But now his mother has died. So we got the signature from one of his assistants."

I look through the doorway and see a fairly young man wiping his brow. He looks as if he has been keelhauled. Ada has somehow compelled him to sign the papers for his boss. I wonder if he will be shot for this. Ada and the brown-haired woman compose themselves and head for the door, signaling to me to come along. I hesitate, feeling sympathy for the deputy. So I blatt him too, handing him a jar of honey, even though there is nothing to be gained from it. Then I scurry after the women.

Events begin to move quickly now. The brown-haired woman peels away from us and returns to her office at flank speed. Ada and I exit the building and head for the cars. There Ada tells Barry and the Duluths to ride with Griescha. None of us has any idea what is going on. Barry is all over me, begging for details. "What happened in there?"

"I think we got the signatures," I tell him. "And I blatted two people."

Ada stuffs Barry and the Duluths into Griescha's car. I watch as they pull away, picturing Barry seated between Rick and Babs, wondering whether he would prefer the death of a thousand cuts.

Ada and I drive off with Pavel. "Where are the others going?" I ask.

"Griescha will take them to a hotel."

"What about me?"

"You have to leave in three days, right?"

"Right."

"Then we'll get you done first."

I realize that my nonchangeable tickets are working in my favor. Their immutability is driving Ada to heroic lengths on my behalf. But this does not prevent me from feeling some soreness of sympathy for the others.

Ada and I drive to a succession of government buildings. In some she chats amiably, in others she argues vociferously. Hell hath no fury like a woman's scorn. In no case do I have the slightest idea what is going on. I am caught up in a vortex of goings and comings and waitings and screamings and dealings and signings. I become hungry and thirsty, yet there is no sign of any pause for refreshment. Ada seems oblivious to the needs of her body. At 6:00 P.M. we drive up a side street to an old stone building, its façade laced with cracks and its interior smelling like a tomb. "Wait here," Ada says when we reach the portico. I watch as she ascends a winding staircase, disappearing into the heights like Moses ascending Sinai. I wonder what truth Ada will be able to bring back to me and whether it will be carved in stone.

The evening has grown cool. For the first time in hours I am not on the move. I have a moment to acknowledge my tiredness, to think of Barry and where he and the Duluths are ensconced. I am still filled with apprehension. Even though things seem to be getting done, I realize that at any point in this chain of events a link may break and all will be lost. I pull my jacket closed about my neck and gaze down the long, dirty street leading from this building. A dog snuffles for scraps in a pile of garbage. Two little girls walk by, arms interlocked, their faces grave, large black bows sprouting from their crowns. A jet roars overhead. A train whistle wails and fades in the distance. Once again I am becoming aware of life around me. Is this because I am letting go of a dream? Have I already accepted the impossibility of this adoption? But why should I? Everything seems to be proceeding apace.

Ada appears from behind. "Any luck?" I ask with no hint of expectation in my voice.

Ada's expression never changes. Either she is holding a three high or a royal flush. "We came here for the passport," she finally divulges. "But a passport can take up to a month."

I have no response to this. It is as if I have long been prepared for the final insult to my credulity. "A month?" I ask, but calmly. "Ada, I don't have a month."

Ada signals me to follow her. We ascend the staircase and enter an office vestibule. "In there," she says, pointing through an open door. I peer inside and see a man in a military uniform standing behind a desk. He is holding a little red booklet and is gently blowing on it, as if drying wet ink. "Go on in," she says, nudging me. I step inside. The officer looks up at me. He snaps the little red booklet shut and hands it to me. Then he shakes my hand and smiles. "Take care of your son."

I open the red booklet and see Alyosha's blank visage staring out at the wide world. My God, this is his passport! Then I look up at the officer and attempt a smile, only I am so awestruck by the breaking of this moment that I cannot manage it. I dig deep into the mire of my Russian vocabulary and finally come up with a feeble "*Spaseeba.*"

Ada leads me out of the building. I walk briskly along behind her, my gaze buried in Alyosha's passport like a Trappist at evensong. We emerge onto the street. "Ada, is he my son?" I ask, needing to hear it again, needing to feel it, needing to have it in braille.

Ada does not even look at me. She is craning her neck for Pavel. "Yes, yes, of course," she says distractedly, as if this is the hundredth adoption she has done this week.

Pavel drives up and Ada and I get in. "Time is short," she says. I sense this too. Perhaps it is only the waning daylight and the advent of the cool evening air. But I feel as if a life is running out, only I do not know whose it is. Within the next few minutes certain landmarks become familiar. We are heading for the orphanage.

By the time we arrive a gentle rain has begun to fall. The land is gray. It casts no shadows because it is a shadow. The sky melds with it and I feel like an apparition moving through this fog of earth and air. Ada and I enter the same low, wooden building where I first met Alyosha. Only this time the place is swarming with children—about forty boys. When they see me they become even more animated, running about, like ants perceiving a threat to the nest. I stand fast, searching, searching the crowd of children. I spot Alyosha on the far side of the room. I raise my hand and he comes tearing at me. He leaps into my arms and I bury my face in the crook of his neck as we exchange bone-crushing hugs. He moves his mouth to my ear. *"Domoi,"* he tells me. "Home."

Alyosha jumps from my arms but remains tight by my side, his small, warm hand clasping mine. Ada shows us to an adjoining room. I help Alyosha out of his sorry threads and into his change of clothes: a pair of jeans, a T-shirt, a Nike hooded sweatshirt. "Do you have shoes?" asks Ada. "I didn't know his size," I tell her. Ada nods resignedly. "Then we will have to borrow them."

After dressing Alyosha I give him a teddy bear—my traveling companion on the flight over. He hugs it to himself. Then I hand him a box of gum. "For your friends," I tell him, pointing to the other kids who have been trying desperately to nose into the room. Alyosha, flush with this responsibility, runs out and distributes the gum. *Spaseeba*s erupt like the whispering of a thousand angels. "We must go," says Ada, but I insist on a group photo. She reluctantly corrals the children into a broad huddle with Alyosha at its focal point. I snap my shot and then another. Alyosha leaps back into my arms, clamping tightly against my chest. I begin to wade slowly through the children. A little boy of about nine reaches out and tugs on my sleeve. His name is Nikolai. He speaks to me; it is an appeal of some kind. I look to Ada; she leans toward me and translates. "Please find me a family in America too." To Ada's frustration, I pause and take his picture. "For Rainbow House," I tell her. "It's the least we can do."

As I reach the door with Alyosha I tell him, through Ada, to say good-bye to his friends. He waves once, then turns his face to the outside world. We set out down the path and he never looks back. But I do. There is a little barefoot boy standing on the threshold, his arms spread wide. He is crying his eyes out. Not because he misses Alyosha, but because, I later learn, Alyosha was given his only pair of shoes.

Alyosha sits next to me in the back seat as we drive to the hotel where Barry and the Duluths are staying. Ada tells me to wait while she goes in and touches base with them. Alyosha and I get out of the car to stretch our legs. No word passes between us, but I cannot take my eyes from him. He is composed and marginally curious about all that is going on, but he never wanders from my side.

There is a call from above. I look up and see Barry leaning out his third-floor window. I hoist Alyosha up to show him off. I am somewhat self-conscious about my having Alyosha in hand while Barry has still not had his happy ending. I can read the mixed feelings playing across Barry's face: He is genuinely happy for me, yet he is thinking, "Why not me?"

Ada returns to the car and tells Pavel to return to Moscow. "What about you?" I ask, swelling with gratitude for what she has done for me. "I need to work with the others now," she says. Her face is weary, but she marches back into the hotel with an air of grim determination.

For most of the return trip to Moscow, Alyosha's face is plastered to the window on his side. It is late—11:00 P.M.—and the lights of villages and passing cars attract his eye. Finally, though, and without a word or a glance toward me, he lays his head down on my lap and sleeps. I recall my red flag from the days of the parenting classes: I get quickly attached to people. My God, at a moment like this how can one help it?

At 1:00 A.M. we arrive at Nellie's apartment in Moscow, where I hand over the orphanage and provincial documents for translation. There is a thick pile of them. It is immediately obvious to me that she will have to work through the night or what little is left of it. "Tomorrow we have to go to the embassy," she reminds me. "But first you'll have to get Alyosha's physical and visa photos done." Then she turns to Alyosha, who is holding my hand, and utters some words of comfort in a desultory fashion. She is tired, Alyosha is tired, and I am beginning to wane as well.

By 2:00 A.M. we are back at the apartment on Potapovsky Prospect. No sooner do I carry Alyosha inside than the babushka is on her feet. She has been sitting at the kitchen table in her bathrobe, fretting. When she sees Alyosha her eyes melt and she buries him in her affections. I watch as she leads him to the kitchen table and, despite the late hour, plies him with tea and crackers while speaking at him nonstop in tones of comfort and welcome and acceptance. Alyosha displays the ritualized manner of the experienced tea drinker, using a spoon to loft his tea to his lips and arranging a set number of crackers within easy reach. By 3:00 A.M. it is truly time for bed. I take Alyosha to the bathroom, give him a toothbrush, toothpaste, washcloth, and soap. I watch as he does his teeth and face, capably and efficiently, and for some reason I am surprised at this. At some level I had expected that he would need me for everything, but he is following patterns of self-care acquired in an institution. For the moment, at least, my role is one of facilitator. I simply point the way and he capably follows.

After Alyosha's ablutions we go to my room. He undresses and I give him one of my T-shirts to sleep in: "Hoboken Classic 5 Mile Run." Then he slips under the covers with his teddy bear. The babushka enters with a book and sits on the edge of the bed, her eyes full of adoration. She opens the book and begins to read him a fairy tale. Her voice is animated yet soothing. Alyosha is riveted to the story. Every so often the babushka pauses and allows him to complete her sentence. I am captivated by this. He is making himself at home and letting people love him. Fifteen minutes into the book Alyosha's eyes are fluttering. A minute later he is out. The babushka retires and I stretch out beside my son. I want to sleep but am afraid to, afraid that if I close my eyes he will vanish. The first feeble rays of the morning sun filter in through the balcony windows. It is by this gentle light that I watch my son's respirations. I count them as long as I can until I too am taken by exhaustion.

—— Friday, July 16, 1993 ——

My alarm sounds at 7:00 A.M. I ease myself out of bed and into a chair, from where I observe my son. He is sleeping on his side with his lovely face resting in his right hand. Sitting here is one of the most satisfying things I have ever done, because Alyosha's sleep lends an aspect of permanence to the moment.

At 7:30 my sense of the advancing day prods me to activity, for there is so much to be done. I wash up, shave, and eat. At 8:15 I return to Alyosha, reluctant to disturb his rest. I nudge him once and then again. He rolls onto his back and awakens with a broad smile. He reaches out and puts his arms around my neck, knowing exactly where he is and who I am.

At mid-morning Pavel comes by to take us for the visa photos. I have dressed Alyosha in jeans, T-shirt, and windbreaker. I give him a small blue backpack, in which he stuffs his teddy bear with only the head sticking out.

With great effort I communicate to Pavel the need to make a stop along the way. The image of that little boy crying, the one who had given his shoes to Alyosha, is weighing heavily on my mind. Pavel takes me to a shoe store. We fight our way through yet another mob of anxious shoppers, and I buy Alyosha a new $4 pair of sneakers. I place his friend's shoes in a bag—after having secreted a pack of chewing gum in one—and give them to Pavel, who will take them to Tula later in the day.

Our next stop is the photographer. After only a few minutes of waiting we are served. Another ten minutes and I am holding the visa photos. It is already 11:00 A.M. Our embassy appointment is at 1:00, and we still have to complete Alyosha's physical, so there is not a moment to spare. Pavel drives us to the Russian clinic. The news that this is an adoption by an American seems to animate the clinicians. Several of the white-coated people look me over and smile. There will be no need for blatt here.

We are led into a small office, where a large, red-faced, older Russian woman is overjoyed to see us. This is the pediatrician, who is grandmotherly in the typically robust Russian fashion and immediately takes Alyosha by the hand. Another doctor is present as well—a translator for the pediatrician, who does not speak a stick of English. The woman is already laughing with Alyosha, and every word she utters bespeaks comfort and concern. She examines my son from head to toe while the other doctor relates the findings to me in English. "He is a little malnourished," he tells me, "but nothing serious. Also a little dehydrated, so give him plenty to drink."

Twenty minutes later the examination is complete. I hand the younger doctor $70, and he rewards me with a sealed envelope containing the details of the examination.

It is now after noon. We are supposed to meet Nellie in front of the embassy, where she will give me all the original documents, plus two official copies of each, plus the certified translations. The traffic is heavy and chaotic, so the going is slow. But we arrive at 12:40, in plenty of time. Nellie is waiting for us by the front entrance. She holds up a large brown envelope and then hands it to me. "This is the last hurdle," she says.

We enter the embassy and take a seat in the same room where the orientation had taken place. There are several other American couples there as well, some of whom I recognize from the orientation session. Now they are all clinging to children, all of them toddlers or infants. Alyosha sits on my lap, not uttering a word. Now and then Nellie leans over to him, whispers something, and he smiles. I notice that a couple across the room is regarding Alyosha with approval. The couple sitting next to me is also looking at him. I overhear the husband say to his wife, "What a handsome boy." I swell with pride. Alyosha *is* strikingly good looking.

I lean over to Nellie and ask her if there is anything I need to know before the interview. She thinks for a moment and then nods. "They will ask Alyosha if he wants to go with you," she tells me. "It is important that he say yes." I do not worry about this, because Alyosha seems uncommonly comfortable with his new status.

But I wonder what would happen if a child was to say no? I broach this question with Nellie. She nods and recalls a recent situation where a boy about Alyosha's age was being adopted by an American couple. The only thing was, he did not want to go. "I won't!" he kept shouting. When asked if he would like to live with those people in America, his answer was immediate: No! Finally, at the embassy as the frantic parents looked on, Nellie convinced the boy that it was important that he answer yes when the embassy official asked him the crucial question. Firming his jaw, he did just that. But as he turned away from the official he declared, "But I really mean *no!*"

At precisely 1:00 P.M. my name is called. I rise and take Alyosha by the hand and over to one of the windows at the counter. My interviewer is the same woman who had given the orientation. She is unsmiling and businesslike. I hand her my package of documents, which she immediately opens and riffles through with a trained eye. She separates the information into discrete piles, removing paper clips here, applying paper clips there. Then, finally, she cracks a thin, bureaucratic smile. "These are nicely done," she says. It is at this moment that I know I am in like Comrade Flynn.

During the course of the next ten minutes she goes through each document and asks me details of their contents. "Do you know what your son's birthday is?" "How long was he in the orphanage?" "Does he have any allergies?" I recognize this as an assessment of my level of interest in my son's background and vital statistics. Fortunately most of the information had already been supplied in a brief from Rainbow House, because I had only a few minutes to gloss over Nellie's translations while waiting for the interview. Finally, the official looks down at Alyosha and begins to speak Russian with him. I am impressed by this—the linguistic ignorance of American foreign-service employees is legendary—and my estimation of this woman immediately rises. She holds a brief conversation with Alyosha, asking him what appears to be a series of questions. He consistently answers, *"Da"*.

"Okay," says the woman, "he understands what is happening here. Everything looks fine."

I look down at Alyosha and squeeze his hand. The woman packages the original documents and the translations and affixes the embassy's seal to the envelope. After I pay the $200 visa fee she hands everything over to me. "Don't open this," she orders. "Just give it to the immigration official in the States."

I take the envelope and my son and return to Nellie. "That's it," she says. "What do you want to do now?"

My head is throbbing from hunger. Alyosha must be hungry too. I offer to treat Nellie to lunch at McDonald's, which is unique in Russia because it actually has something called "service." Nellie is keen on the idea, and the three of us head out.

Alyosha is wide-eyed as we make our way through crowded Moscow. It is his first time riding a subway, and he laughs as the automatic doors slide open before him. The escalator is a revelation. It takes him two or three tries before he learns how to mount it in a smooth fashion, after which he wants to ride it again and again.

The McDonald's is bright, expansive, and crowded. I order a cheeseburger, a Sprite, and fries for Alyosha, whose eyes are already feasting on the pop-American staples. He spends a lot of time sucking and blowing soda with his straw. Nellie observes this and turns to me. "He has never used a straw before," she says. When we get up to leave, Alyosha lovingly places the straw in his backpack. "He wants to keep it," she remarks.

Nellie sees us safely back to the apartment and then takes leave of us. "We're hoping that Barry and Babs and Rick get their children today," she says. "I have to be ready to do their translations too."

Alyosha naps in the afternoon. He gets up at about 3:30 and then spends more than an hour on the jungle gym in the vestibule. I watch with the satisfaction of the proud father as he swings with practiced skill among the bars and ropes. This is the wonder of adopting an older child. So many skills are already in place, some honed to a remarkable degree. One by one they will present themselves to me, and I will be duly amazed.

The babushka serves us supper—eggs, cabbage soup, and cold cuts. Alyosha eats ravenously, and then he has his ritual tea. After supper we go for a short walk down Potapovsky Prospect. I buy him a Mars bar. We return home, play on the jungle gym, and draw some pictures. Around 8:00 P.M. I indicate to him that I want him to take a bath. He offers modest opposition. As I get him into the tub, I am aware that the babushka is watching me. I soap up a washcloth and begin to administer my son's first bath. The babushka enters the bathroom, observes me for a moment, and clucks her tongue. The next thing I know, she has relieved me and shoved me onto the threshold. She takes up the washcloth and begins to abrade Alyosha from head to toe. I was obviously being too gentle. It is as if she is saying, "This is dirt. Dirt! You've got to *scrub!*" Despite my chagrin, I am grateful for the unremitting love she shows him.

By 9:00 Alyosha is in bed. The babushka reads to him again and he revels in the story, his eyes bright with attention. But the day soon catches up with him and he falls off to sleep. I stay up and read until 10:00; then I turn in as well. There is nothing else to be done. No more papers, no more officials, no more hurdles of any kind. After two weeks in Russia, tomorrow, my last day, will be free of any external responsibilities. I will be able to simply enjoy myself with my son.

My deep, resonant sleep is soon shattered. A door opens and slams. A child wails. There are footfalls in the vestibule. I jump out of bed and into my pants. Shirtless, I run toward the silhouettes that play on the frosted glass of the bedroom door. When I emerge into the vestibule, Barry is hurrying through, followed closely by Ada and Griescha. The babushka is up and cooking, and Igor, by some magic, has rematerialized. I greet my friend, who is holding his little girl. She is hysterical, but her ululations are a clarion call and a fresh invigoration for the babushka, who takes the child and rocks her, cooing and speaking softly to her as she somehow frees a hand to make her something to eat.

Barry pauses to say good-bye and thank you to Ada and Griescha. Then he gives me all the details, which closely match my own experience. I am happy for his success. Now the chapter is truly coming to a close. Barry, Igor, and I crowd into the kitchen with the babushka and Katya. We surround the frightened child and watch as the babushka delivers tiny spoonfuls of pablum to her. She is quiet now, but the quivering of her lip bespeaks a readiness to lose control at any moment. Barry asks about Alyosha and I tell him everything is fine.

Everything really is fine. I realize that if I was not so tired it would be almost too much to bear.

—— Saturday, July 17, 1993 ——

An absolutely unencumbered day. No appointments, no documents to be signed, no fees to be paid.

Alyosha and I rise late and have breakfast together at the babushka's kitchen table. I am consistently amazed at my son's great ease in his new situation. He radiates an assumption that where he is is where he is supposed to be and who he is with is the person he is supposed to be with. He takes his tea, explores the apartment, and plays in the jungle gym, in the complete confidence that when he emerges from these activities I will be there for him. It is as if he carries his own quiet, controlled space about himself, and when he approaches, he includes me within its borders as well.

I sense neither grief nor fear in his aspect. He readily takes my hand and periodically crawls into my lap with a soupçon of possessiveness about the act. For the moment he is my perfect son—it is as if we were programmed for one another in a previous life.

Towards noon we go out for a walk. Alyosha has never been in the capital of his country, yet it seems slightly presumptuous for me to assume the role of tour guide when I do not even speak the language. Alyosha is interested in his surroundings, but not overwhelmed by the crowds, the traffic, and the effusion of goods lining the streets. His eyes sparkle with life—it is that same look of engagement I saw when he was analyzing the workings of the Pez dispenser. As we pass yet another sidewalk card table holding a pyramid of Mars Bars, he points, first to the candy and then to his mouth. I make the purchase, hand it to him, and we walk on. Fifteen minutes later we pass another display of the same candy and he asks for more. I shake my head, point to his belly, and show him a pained expression. Alyosha looks at me, firms his jaw, and pulls his hand from mine. Then he makes a comment, which, from the key words I am able to understand, is something like, "Then I won't hold your hand anymore."

The power struggle has begun.

Five minutes later, under the subtle pressure of competing for space on the sidewalk, Alyosha's hand snakes its way into mine again, and we press on, first to the Kremlin, then to Lenin's tomb, where we watch the changing of the guard with Alyosha sitting high atop my shoulders. Lastly, we pay a sidewalk photographer to take our picture in front of St. Basil's Cathedral. For three dollars I receive a photo of a slightly discontented Alyosha (the denial of that second Mars Bar!) being held by his close-eyed father.

With Alyosha by my side I am finally able to love being where I am. I relish being part of this crowd, I listen intently to the Russian of passing conversations, allowing it to fill my ears, and I watch with delight as kerchiefed babushkas haggle over the prices of fruits and vegetables. In less than twenty-four hours we will be airborne, leaving a place I am only just now getting to know. Most of my days here have been spent in desperate apprehension, filled with anxiety. If I did not know better I would say that this whole experience had been carefully orchestrated—the initial manic activity of settling in and receiving instructions, the presentation of a set schedule, the ensuing panic and depression in the face of incipient failure, and, finally, redemption in the form of my son. The show is now over, and I am given one worry-free day in Moscow as a sort of battle award. But I have to work hard to be so cynical. It no longer comes easy, nor should it. This is my moment of greatest joy. I do not want any more than what I now have. This is as good as it gets. This is enough.

— Sunday, July 18, 1993 —

Sleep is almost impossible. Not only are we going to travel in a few hours, we are going to abandon a world and a way of life. It seems unnatural that in so short a time we will be compelled to emotionally let go of Russia in order to move to the rhythms of a completely different reality, a place where only English is spoken and all the telephones work.

At 5:00 A.M. I get up, shave, and wash. At 5:30 I rouse Alyosha. After all that I have been through, it is strange to acknowledge the existence of this moment, a moment that had so often threatened to remain a fantasy. My heart is almost breaking. Not because I will particularly miss anything here in Russia, but because Alyosha cannot possibly understand the nature and degree of the changes he is about to undergo. He is committing the ultimate act of trust: placing his life and future in my hands. Does he think America is just another part of Russia? Does he know he will never live here again? The essence of Russianness — the soulful response to the complications of living — is something he will never know in full blossom. Yet he harbors a piece of it: in the delight he takes in the smallest gift and his ready acknowledgment of the most incidental gestures of kindness. Will American pop culture and its controlling influences supplant this beautiful aspect of his ethnicity? Right now he sings along with Russian cartoons of dancing alligators and their sweet-hearted companions. In America he will find "Beavis and Butthead."

The babushka serves us our final breakfast: tea and those little pancakes. I can barely touch the food, but Alyosha eats heartily. Barry gets up to spend a few, final moments with us. I can hear every metallic tick of the kitchen clock as the hands push on toward 6:00, 6:15, 6:30. There is a knock at the door. Pavel enters and immediately takes our bags, which are packed and waiting for him in the vestibule. His sense of urgency motivates all of us. The babushka begins to weep in a manner that perceives every leave-taking as a death. Igor too looks shaken. He presents me with a souvenir copy of a Russian icon. "Put it near his bed," he directs me.

I bid farewell to Barry; we promise to stay in touch. We must, for we are the only two who are truly privy to what went on here.

Alyosha takes his teddy bear. I help him with his little blue backpack, which I have stuffed with jigsaw puzzles, crayons, and a box of Cracker Jack. He takes my hand and, largely untouched by the emotion of the moment, follows along.

Pavel packs us into the back of his Lada. I press my face against the window and look up at the crumbling apartment building on Potapovsky Prospect. We drive off and are soon heading for the airport at high speed. As we move down the highway, my mind is unwinding, playing back in a jumbled fashion the images of my two weeks here. Life is so complicated for these Russians; but because of this, the simplest comforts bring profound joy. For a moment I shudder when I consider how the excesses of economic reform may affect these people.

When we arrive at the airport, Pavel wastes no time in bidding us farewell. I blatt him, with cash, and watch as he pats Alyosha's cheek and speaks some words to him. It is as if he is saying farewell forever to one of his own children.

Alyosha and I muscle our way aboard our Aeroflot flight with a magnificent herd of Russians. This is the last step in the adoption—the brute physical act of getting on the plane. I show Alyosha to the window seat and take my place next to him. We strap ourselves in while most of the other passengers are still afoot, stowing boxes and plastic bags and cheap vinyl duffles in overhead compartments and under seats. The plane is full, with not a seat to spare. The temperature is stultifying and every surface feels sticky. The only creature comfort is the absence of a single evangelist.

When we begin to taxi down the runway, Alyosha leans into the window and begins to talk animatedly in Russian, looking back at me with a presumption of my total comprehension. As we pick up speed he sits back in his seat and slips his hand into mine. Finally, this huge machine noses up and I feel the wheels leave Russian soil. Now they cannot possibly have him back.

We follow the same flight route: Moscow to New York via Shannon and Gander. I buy Alyosha a juice here, an ice cream there. In Newfoundland his eyes brighten when he sees the galaxy of goods in the duty-free shop. He points out a Matchbox car and I buy it on the spot.

The flight home is just as long as the flight to Russia: fifteen hours. Alyosha sleeps, plays with his puzzles, occasionally speaks to me. When I gesture my lack of understanding, he smiles and waves a dismissive hand, as if I must be kidding. I cannot take my eyes from him. Every moment is charged with a boundless love for this little boy. But there is also an undercurrent of disbelief: that he is really here and he is really mine. I watch as Alyosha puts his puzzles away and lays his head down on my lap. It has taken me twenty-eight months to adopt a child. There are moments when I am filled with heart-wrenching lament when I consider how much sooner I could have had Alyosha had I only known of him. But such thoughts, when they do arise, are fleeting. Mercifully so. I am amazed at how little inclination I have to dwell on the painful and bitter aspects of my adoption experience. The advent of my son has suddenly forced me to lean into the future, like the figurehead of a tall ship. Because we have only just begun our life together, I can only presume that the best days for both of us lie ahead, in a land brimming with bubblegum and other good things. It has been said that one begins to feel old when memories mean more than plans. With Alyosha in my life now, I see horizons unlimited. And I have never felt so young.

Epilogue

I never received the partial refund Jorge had promised nor did I hear from Marilyn again *(Caveat emptor)*. Perhaps I should be grateful for their misdemeanors, for without them I would never have found the son I now have.

It has been almost six years since I adopted Alyosha. The curious, energetic seven year old is now in the full flower of his thirteenth year. I do not often think of Alyosha as being adopted. I feel as if I have raised him all his life, but just can't seem to find his baby pictures.

I had mentioned that Russian children released for foreign adoption must be considered "unadoptable" by Russian nationals by virtue of some physical or behavioral shortcoming. Alyosha's turned out to be his age: As a seven year old he fell solidly into the camp of the older child. His "disability" in Russian eyes proved to be my very good fortune.

When we arrived home in Maine, Alyosha took full command of his environment. He immediately converted his bed into a trampoline, bounding on it until I had to restrain him and direct his energies elsewhere. This was an auspicious start to his life in a new country, for Alyosha has continued to be a happy and well-adjusted child.

Have there been difficulties? Yes, but nothing out of the ordinary. The language was the first big hurdle, of course. During the first couple of months I was often on the phone to native Russian speakers who lived nearby, asking them to translate for either me or my son—especially at the very beginning when I could not seem to prepare foods that appealed to his palate. But by the third month, Alyosha was making great strides in expressing himself with his pigeonized English.

Once, after rolling around with him in the backyard, he straddled my lap and threw me an inquisitive look. "Papa," he asked, "where mama?"

Totally unmanned by this question, I tried to gather my thoughts for a reply he would understand. But before I could begin, Alyosha patted me on the cheek, nodding and smiling. "That okay," he said. "Papa mama."

No truer words were ever spoken. If there is any longer such a thing as male and female roles, for the single parent they have no meaning. I am disciplinarian, playmate, homework tutor, and chauffeur as well as seamstress, cook, nurse, and soccer mom. Still, Alyosha has had the benefit of interacting with strong, affirming women. I have been especially fortunate in that his teachers (females all until the fifth grade) have always been the right ones at the right time.

A case in point is when Alyosha entered second grade shortly after his arrival. Undoubtedly feeling out of place with his limited language abilities, it was often a struggle to bring him to school. For the first couple of months I had to sit with him for half an hour or so until he collected himself to the point where he could go it alone for the rest of the day. Still, as I walked away from the building, I would often turn back to see him standing with his face pressed against the window, a last gentle tear making its way down his cheek, his hand raised in a poignant gesture of farewell.

Returning to school one day to pick him up, I found his teacher seated in her easy chair, rocking a tearful Alyosha in her arms. Mrs. White looked up at me and quietly whispered, "He said he misses Russia." Her sensitivity and support were there when I could not be, and I've always been grateful for this.

The fascinating thing about adopting an older child is that both personality and basic abilities are already in place and fairly well developed. I discovered early that although Alyosha was cheerful, honest, and affectionate, he was also very independent minded. As a result, I vowed at the outset never to get into a head-to-head argument with him, for such would allow only two possible outcomes: either I would lose or I would become irrational. Diplomacy, once again, has been everything.

As for his abilities, he is skilled at mathematics and art (a wonderful combination) and is a natural athlete. In the third grade, when he stepped out onto the basketball court for the first time, I was amazed at his ball-handling skills. Another parent tapped me on the shoulder and remarked, "Where did he learn to play like that?" I could only gulp and stare in wonder. "I don't know," I said, adding, "he certainly doesn't get it from me."

Alyosha speaks of his future with confidence and anticipation. His dream, at the moment, is to be a professional soccer player and middle-school math teacher. He also sometimes speaks of the past. I am always surprised at the clarity and detail with which he recalls his life in Russia.

Still, I dwell relatively little on the future, for it is Alyosha's genial and loving companionship, as well as his needs and experiences, that anchor me securely in the present. During the day, when I am in my school and Alyosha in his, I miss him. When he comes home with a drawing he has dedicated to me, I am warmed to know that he was thinking of me as well. In this way, we are making the most of the life that we have, in the moment at hand. This bodes favorably, I hope, for happiness in the future as well.